FUCHSIAS

■ For House and Garden ■

George Bartlett

CROWOOD GARDENING GUIDES

First published in 1990 by
The Crowood Press Ltd
Ramsbury, Marlborough
Wiltshire SN8 2HR

This impression 1994

British Library Cataloguing-in-Publication Data

Bartlett, George 1929–,
    Fuchsias; for house and garden
    1. Gardens, Fuchsias, Cultivation
    I. Title
    635.9'3344

    ISBN 1 85223 259 5

Picture Credits
All cover photographs by Carl Wallace. Front cover is Blush o'Dawn, back
cover (top) is Michele Wallace, and back cover (bottom) is Paula Jane.
Frontispiece photograph is Snowcap.
All colour photographs by Carl Wallace, except on page 4 and Figs 6, 64,
66, 68, 69, 71, 72, 118, 119, 120, 121, 122, 123, 124, and 125, by Dave
Pike. Thanks to Tony Luker.
Line drawings by Claire Upsdale-Jones.

Typeset by Acorn Bookwork, Salisbury, Wiltshire.
Printed and bound by Paramount Printing Group, Hong Kong

Contents

Introduction

Although I have been growing fuchsias since 1966 I often wonder whether a 'health warning' ought to be given as an introduction to any book on the subject. The problem is that, once you embark upon the journey of fuchsia growing, it is extremely hard to give it up. Addiction might be too strong a word to use, but certainly once the 'bug' has bitten it will only be with considerable difficulty that a cure can be effected. To say that fuchsia growers become fanatical would be incorrect, but there is always the temptation to grow just a few more and before long all other horticultural interests are pushed to one side.

Why is there so much interest in this one genus of plants? What is the fascination with a simple flower like the fuchsia? The last question probably gives us a clue to the answer – simplicity. The fuchsia is simple in two ways – in its shape and form, and in its cultivation. Those who have had the pleasure of seeing the hedges of fuchsias growing wild in Ireland or in the west of England long remember the way in which they seem to glow in the sunlight. It is only when a closer examination is made of this mass of red and purple that each individual flower reveals its simplicity. As to their cultivation – the other reason for their popularity – there is nothing very difficult about growing fuchsias. They can be grown in many different ways and used for many different purposes. There are many differing cultivars to choose from, and their varying sizes, colour and form give a perpetual kaleidoscope from which it is difficult to detach yourself. Fuchsias are easy to grow and to propagate. They can be grown in all types of conditions, and they will usually do well whatever we do to them. There is no one set of rules which must be obeyed in order to produce a beautiful plant – rules, if made, can be broken and yet still the flowers shake their heads and continue to flourish.

Within this book I have attempted to pass on some of the enthusiasm I have for the fuchsia, and tried to lead the novice along a path which will ensure better than moderate success. I hope that with the beautiful pictures and line drawings you will be encouraged to grow more of my favourite plants and will want to become involved in those societies which concentrate on promoting the growing of fuchsias.

If, as a result of the success I am sure you will achieve, you wish to become involved with growing plants to be seen on the show benches then I wish you all good luck. My main object, though, is to encourage you to grow your plants for fun and to enjoy growing them. You can brighten the area where you live with a mass of glorious fuchsia blooms and, by passing on pieces of plants for propagation, encourage your neighbours to do the same.

I am certainly grateful to have the opportunity to share my enthusiasm and fun with you.

George Bartlett

CHAPTER 1

Beginning

OBTAINING YOUR FIRST PLANT

From a Friend

The greatest number of converts to the pleasure of growing fuchsias probably come about as a result of friendship. One of the fuchsia's main attributes is its ability to create a new plant from a piece detached from an existing plant. Growers of fuchsias rapidly realise just how easy it is to 'root' cuttings, and many new plants are produced and then passed on to friends. The motto of the British Fuchsia Society is 'Fuchsia folk are friendly folk', but perhaps it is the flower itself which is the friendlier!

From a Shop

From early spring onwards fuchsia plants, many in full flower, go on offer in shops. Are plants bought early in the year good buys? Much will depend upon the conditions available to you as to whether plants should be bought in, say, April or May, but in general you should avoid buying any fuchsia plant which is in flower at so early a date. Fuchsias should not really be in flower until the beginning of July, and some even think that July is rather early. So, how do the growers of these flowering plants manage to produce them so early in the year? What special treatment is necessary and is it possible for the ordinary 'man in the street' to emulate these conditions? In order to flower, a fuchsia needs to be a mature plant and needs to have been living in 'short night' conditions. To ensure the plant's maturity, considerable heat and light are given to it early in

the year – during the winter in fact. To encourage flowering, the length of the 'night' is shortened by using lighting, and the plants grow, therefore, in ideal but false conditions. It is difficult to reproduce such conditions, and many of the willing buyers of these plants are often extremely disappointed when the plants lose their flowers and drop their buds soon after being placed in their new quarters.

So, should you buy from shops? Of course – many excellent plants are available – but do leave your buying of fuchsias until they are correctly in season, that is, from July onwards. That way you will be able to give them the type of conditions in which they will thrive.

In the spring it is also possible to purchase from shops young rooted cuttings, or well-grown young plants which are not yet showing buds. These, especially if they are correctly named, are often excellent buys and are to be recommended. Such plants can be used in many different ways – in the garden, in pots, in troughs, in patio tubs or in baskets. In fact, if you have greenhouse conditions, early spring is an excellent time of the year to buy young plants from shops and garden centres, but do choose them carefully.

From a Nursery

Without doubt the best way to purchase plants is by choosing them at a specialist fuchsia nursery – you will probably find the names of those local to you by examining the pages of gardening papers. You will be able to make your selection from a vast number of clearly-named plants, and you will also be able to decide, especially if you

Fig 1   Fuchsia stem with flower and foliage.

obtain a copy of the nursery catalogue before your visit, precisely which plants you wish to acquire and the purpose for which you wish to grow them. In most nurseries the plants will be set out in alphabetical order and there will be long rows of individual cultivars. You will, therefore, have the opportunity to choose the strongest of the cultivars.

You should be warned, however, that there will be a great temptation to buy many more plants than you originally intended, and you will probably have to be very firm with yourself. Have a list prepared well in advance – decide how many of each cultivar you will require, remembering that a basket will look much better if it contains a number of the same

7

Fig 2   The front of a house decorated with fuchsias and mixed flowers.

cultivar. You might even consider sending your list to the nursery in advance of your visit so that they can be ready for you on arrival. Although this will rob you of the opportunity to choose the strongest for yourself, you will probably find that the nurseryman will select those he considers the best for you.

At nurseries it is also possible to choose between 'rooted cuttings' and 'small plants'. The former will need extra care once you get them home, but they will be slightly cheaper. Usually it is better to go for the latter – young plants which will probably already have been 'stopped', and will thus be producing their first branches.

Perhaps the most important advantage of visiting a nursery to buy your plants is the opportunity you have to talk to the person who has raised them. A discussion (always freely and willingly given in nurseries), will tell you the type of compost that has been used, and give you advice on how to get the best from the growing plants. Also, it is possible to visit such nurseries from January onwards, so, provided you have the right conditions at home, you will have a head start with your young plants. Rooted cuttings bought in February, March or April will produce fine flowering specimens growing in 5–6in (13–15cm) pots from July onwards. Plants will also have achieved the right type of growth for planting out in the garden from the beginning of June.

Fig 3   'Stanley Cash', a double-flowered fuchsia.

Through the Post

If you glance through the gardening publications you will see a vast number of addresses from which it is possible to obtain young fuchsia plants. Many of the descriptions given, and the prices charged, will encourage growers to send for the plants or collections offered, but this is one method of buying which should be considered carefully – not because the quality of goods on offer is likely to be poor, but because any young plants enclosed in a box, completely without light and moisture for a number of days, are likely to suffer a setback. Do not be tempted to go for the cheapest plants or collections on offer – they are usually cheaper because the quality of the packing is inferior. Many of the specialist fuchsia nurseries send their plants in specially-designed boxes, and very often by rail. Such plants usually arrive in excellent condition.

My honest opinion would be, buy through the post if you must, but please remember that your plants will need very careful attention when they arrive. Dissatisfaction with the quality of the goods received should always be reported back immediately to the nursery concerned. Delays, often not of their making, are frequently the cause of the dissatisfaction.

FIRST STEPS

Having obtained your very first plant, the anxious question arises as to what you should now do with it. There can be no simple answer to this, as much will depend upon the size of the plant,

Fig 4   'Marin Glow'.

Fig 5   Fuchsia cuttings being grown on.

the type of pot in which it is growing, and the time of the year.

Small Rooted Cuttings

Very often when you receive small rooted cuttings through the post they will be wrapped in moist paper, as it is less costly to send them this way than by including the pot and a quantity of compost. Whether the cutting is in a pot or in paper, it should be dealt with in the same way. Consider always that the plants, since rooting, have received a traumatic shock, and treat them very carefully indeed.

You will need a quantity of small pots, preferably no larger than 3in (7.5cm) in diameter – if you have some small 2½in (6cm) square pots, these are ideal. You will also need some compost. There are many good peat-based composts available, such as Levington Potting Compost, Arthur Bowers, or Humber. These

are all ideal, but if you have another favourite type, do use it. Peat-based composts are well balanced, with sufficient nutritional value to keep your plants happy for a few weeks, and they are often more reliable than loam-based composts. However, if you like using a loam-based compost, and can guarantee getting a good fresh supply, it will be no problem – fuchsias will grow quite happily in whatever compost you choose.

Make sure that you keep each label in close proximity to each cutting so that there is no possibility of them becoming mixed up. Use plastic labels, with either a marking pen or a pencil.

Now you are ready to examine your new plants. Carefully remove the paper and any old compost that may still be adhering to the roots. Spread the young white roots out, and remove with scissors any that are damaged or appear brown in colour. Dealing with each young cutting one at a time, place a small quantity of your

11

compost in the base of the pot, gently hold the cutting over the pot and carefully spread the roots so that they are evenly spaced over the compost. Holding the cutting centrally with one hand, trickle compost into the pot with the other. Do not firm the compost at all but let it settle around the roots by gently tapping the pot on your table or bench. Place the label in the pot and you will have completed your first potting. When you have dealt with all your cuttings in the same way, place all the pots on a tray or the staging of a greenhouse and, using the fine rose on a watering can, gently water the plants. This watering will firm the compost around the roots of the cuttings.

These young plants will have received quite a shock to the system, so it is important to give them preferential treatment for a while. They will not appreciate dry heat, so keep them fairly cool and protected from the sun by covering them – I find that a single sheet of newspaper placed over the plants is very satisfactory. This will keep them shaded and will, at the same time, create a pleasant moist atmosphere around the cuttings, to help to keep them turgid until the roots have the opportunity of starting to take up moisture from the compost. It might be a good idea to look at the plants on a daily basis and give them a gentle overhead spraying with slightly tepid pure water. After approximately a week the roots will have started to work their way around the compost and the shading can be removed. This advice applies equally, whether you have a greenhouse or whether you are growing your cuttings initially on an indoor window-sill.

Assuming your cuttings are obtained during the spring, the temperature in which the young plants are placed is critical – the ideal will be in the vicinity of 50°F (10°C). At this type of temperature the young plants will start to grow away quite rapidly. If you are caring for the cuttings in a greenhouse, and you do not wish to heat the whole of the house to this temperature, it might be as well to provide yourself with a small propagator which can give the necessary temperature and protection. Consideration might also be given to partitioning off a small area of your greenhouse, and heating that to the required temperature. In the early part of the year the essential is to make sure that the plants do not suffer from excessive cold. Below a temperature of 40°F (about 5°C), the young plants will feel decidedly chilly and will not grow.

If the young plants are brought in during early summer, your major cause for concern will be shading from too hot a sun. This is an easy task which can be accomplished by using sheets of newspaper.

Young Plants from Nurseries

When good young plants or rooted cuttings are obtained from specialist fuchsia nurseries, it is probable (in fact, almost certain) that each will be growing in its own individual pot, and for this reason the young plant should suffer no setback when you transfer it to your own premises. One word of warning is that if your new acquisitions have been growing in ideal, warm and humid conditions, transferring them to the back of a cold car could be upsetting. Make preparations before leaving for the nursery to ensure that your purchases will remain snug and warm – a cardboard box insulated with newspapers will help to keep out the cold, as will a seed tray propagator with its plastic dome. Perhaps the most important thing to remember is that once you have purchased your plants you should make all speed to get them home and in the comfort of your own accommodation.

Once home, examine your plants carefully. Leave them in the pots in which they are growing for a week or two, placing them in conditions similar to those in which they were growing in the nursery. Keep them, for a few days at least, in your own propagator so that the humidity surrounding them is fairly high. Spray them overhead regularly (as opposed to watering them), so that the compost they are in remains just moist. If you have a collection of plants already it is not a bad idea to keep your

Fig 6   A small greenhouse and pot-grown fuchsias.

new ones segregated from the rest for two or three weeks, just in case they have an infection which could be passed on – it is not unknown even for specialist fuchsia nurseries to suffer from the debilitating disease called 'rust'. Any infection on your new plants should become visible within that span of time.

Some fuchsia nurseries root their young plants in peat pots. These pots are excellent, but they do cause some growers (even experienced ones!) anxiety. If you have ever purchased these peat pots you will have read the instructions which advise you to soak the pots thoroughly before using them. This soaking causes the pots to become sufficiently soft for young roots to penetrate the sides. There have been complaints that the peat pots harden and prevent roots from penetrating, but this can only happen when moisture is leached out of the pots, and they become dry. This can be prevented. If you

have bought young plants rooted in these pots completely immerse the pots in water, thoroughly soaking them – if you can do this overnight it will be especially beneficial. Do not attempt to remove the peat pot when transferring the plant into a plastic pot. Take a 3½in (9cm) plastic pot, place a small quantity of your compost in the base, stand your peat-potted plant on this and completely fill the sides so that the surplus completely covers the peat pot. No part of the peat pot should be visible – if it is, the air will dry the moisture from the peat pot causing it to dry out completely and go hard. Once filled, your new pot should be watered well and should subsequently be kept moister than is usually recommended. By using this method the roots will grow through the peat pot, which will disintegrate fairly quickly and will become part of the compost in your new pot.

CHAPTER 2

Basics

COMPOST

There is no magical compost formula which will guarantee success when growing plants, but we fuchsia growers are lucky, as the needs of the fuchsia are minimal. What type of compost is it therefore best to use? Basically, if you are happy with the type of compost you usually use when growing other pot plants – perhaps John Innes potting or seed composts – and you can guarantee being able to obtain good fresh supplies, use them for your fuchsias. The John Innes formulae have proved very successful over the years, especially when used in conjunction with clay pots. The loam base of this compost is heavier, and with the porosity of clay pots sufficient air will permeate to assist in the aeration of the roots.

Similarly, if you like using the Levington potting composts, and are successful with them, then use them for your fuchsias. These are peat-based composts and will therefore be more suitable when used in conjunction with plastic pots. They are well balanced with regard to fertilisers and your fuchsias will thrive in them.

Arthur Bowers is another of the well-known peat-based composts often used by successful growers. If the consistency of this compost suits your style of growing, use it for your fuchsias.

The Humber Potting Compost is the one I personally use and recommend. It too is a peat-based compost, although it does contain a certain amount of loam and rather more grit than most other similar composts.

If you mix your own compost, and are happy with the results, continue to do so – there is much to be said for this practice. It probably works out slightly cheaper and it does not require a great deal of effort. You will need peat, sharp sand and a compost base – the latter can be easily obtained, and I would recommend Chempak Potting Base. When all the ingredients have been well and truly mixed (6 × 2-gallon (9-litre) buckets of peat; 2 × 2-gallon (9-litre) buckets of sharp sand, grit or perlite; potting base) you have a good fresh compost which will be ready for use after twenty-four hours.

Various elements make a compost suitable for fuchsias. Basically, fuchsias require a compost which has the ability to hold moisture and nutrient but which is also well drained. Fuchsias like to have a moistness around their roots but do not want to be standing in a wet mess. I prefer to err on the side of excessive drainage and am prepared to add further grit, sharp sand or perlite.

Don't be tempted to get a pot full of earth from the garden. Many people are, and they are very often disappointed with the results achieved. This is a method not to be recommended, even if you have only one or two plants.

POTTING

Every gardener must bear in mind that restricting the roots of any plant in a container is completely unnatural. In the garden, or in the wild, the roots are free to roam at will in their search for the nutrients necessary to maintain the vigorous growth of the plant. We must therefore consider the needs of the plant and the desire of those roots to forage. One aspect which is most important is that there can only be growth of the top foliage of any plant if there is movement and growth of the roots. If the roots are restricted and cannot grow, or the source of food within a container has been completely exhausted, the plant will feel threatened and will do what nature intends – that is, produce seeds as quickly as possible to ensure the continuation of the species. To produce its seeds it must first produce its flowers. When that happens, growth of the foliage will slow down or perhaps even stop. Gardeners make use of nature's need to produce seeds to encourage their plants to flower as and when they require.

When considering what type of container to use for your plants, you should look only at those which have drainage holes in the base through which excess water can pass. Fuchsias need a good, well-drained compost so undrained containers will be of little use. The two types of flower pots usually used by growers of fuchsias are made of plastic and clay. When deciding upon which is the better, much depends on the type of compost you prefer to use. A peat-based compost, which tends to dry out more quickly than a loam-based one, will be more suitable for use with plastic pots. Conversely, a loam-based compost is more appropriate when using the more porous clay pots. Having said that, growers using either type of pot with all types of compost still produce good results, and experience will show the right pot and compost for you.

The size of the pot used will depend a great deal upon the size of the plant and its root formation. A young cutting about 2in (5cm) high would look lost in a 6in (15cm) pot, and the small root system would be surrounded by a great deal of unused compost – it would be rather like putting a young baby in a large double bed! You should get used to planting in pots which will just comfortably take the root system.

When your cuttings have rooted they should be carefully separated from their compatriots (if more than one have been rooted together), and placed in a pot not exceeding 3in (7.5cm) in

Fig 7   Potting on from propagation pots to 3in (7.5cm) pots.

diameter. Some growers at this stage wash away all the compost from the roots so that when potted the young plant will be in completely new compost. If the cuttings have been rooted separately there is no need to carry out this task.

Potting plants is an art, and one that improves with practice. A quantity of your fresh compost should be placed in the base of the pot, the rooted cutting held centrally with one hand whilst fresh compost is allowed to trickle around the roots until the pot has been filled. A tap on the bench will settle the compost around the root system, and the task can be completed by watering with the fine rose on a watering can. I would never advise firming the compost around the root system with your fingers or thumbs. Let the watering do the firming for you.

For the compost to be able to 'trickle', it should be just moist in texture. If it is too wet it will be lumpy, and if it is too dry, although it will 'trickle', it will be difficult to moisten later. To test the compost for the right state of moistness take a handful in one hand and squeeze it. If moisture oozes from it it is too wet, and if when the hand is opened the compost falls to pieces it is too dry.

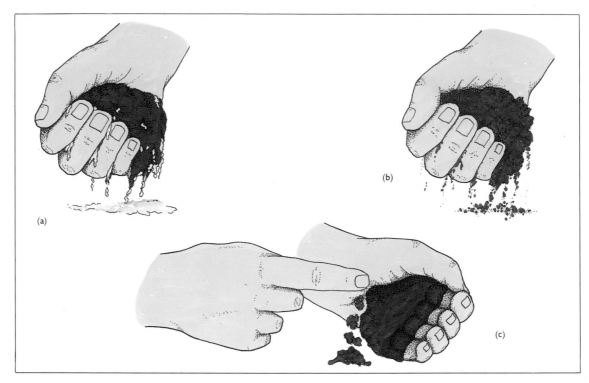

Fig 8   (a) If there is moisture oozing between the fingers when you take a
handful of compost, the compost is too wet. (b) If a handful of compost does
not retain the shape of the hand, and crumbles, it is too dry and needs
moistening. (c) When a handful of compost retains the shape of the hand,
but crumbles when it is touched, it is sufficiently moist and ready for use.

If it retains the shape of the closed hand and only
separates when poked with a finger, then it is
correct.

When the pot in which you have placed your
young plant has become filled with roots it is
time to move your plant into a larger pot. 'Filled
with roots' is probably the incorrect thing to say.
Examine the rootball regularly by inverting the
flower pot and letting the compost and roots
rest upon your hand. If fresh young white roots
are readily visible through the compost at the
sides of the pot, and roots have reached the
bottom, then it is time to 'pot on'. Do not wait
until the roots are circling the compost as they
will have difficulty later in working through the
new compost.

Transferring the plants from a 3in (7.5cm) pot
into a 4in (10cm) or 5in (13cm) pot can be
carried out in the normal way. However, there is
an easier way, with less possibility of getting
compost on the lower foliage. Place a small
quantity of compost in the base of the new pot.
Take a pot of the same size as that in which the
plant is growing, and place it on this compost.
Using fresh, just moist compost, fill the pot within
the pot to overflowing. Continue to pour in
more compost until the new pot is completely
full, and then tap the new pot on the bench to
settle the compost. The rim of the smaller pot
should be visible, and you now remove this,
without disturbing the compost, to be left with a
moulded shape, the exact size of the pot in
which the plant has been growing. Remove your
plant from its old pot and gently drop it into the

Fig 9 'Mieke Meursing'.

hole. A tap on the bench and the job is completed – without fuss or messy compost all over the place.

Each time you 'pot on' your plant you can use this method and there will be no root disturbance at all. The plant will continue to grow healthily, with its roots searching out the nutrients contained in the new compost.

What size pot should you be aiming for in the first season? A cutting taken in February or March should finish up in a pot of either 5in (13cm) or 6in (15cm) in its first season, where it will flower quite happily. Plants which have been over-wintered and which started in 3½in (9cm) pots or even 5in (13cm) pots at the beginning of the season can grow to a much larger size and will probably need 7, 8 or 9in (17.5, 20 or 22.5cm) pots or tubs. Try to get your plant in a pot proportional to its size.

If you are training your plants to grow as standards it is important to keep moving the plants into larger pots so that there is room for the root growth which will encourage top

Fig 10   Transferring a plant to a bigger size of pot by making a 'mould' with a pot the same size as the original.

Fig 11   'Mieke Meursing' in a 5in (12.5cm) pot.

growth. If the pot is full of roots before the required height is reached, the plant, feeling threatened, will start to produce its flower buds and upward growth will cease.

There are two reasons why you should go to the trouble of gradually 'potting on' from one pot to another. The first and most obvious is that a very large pot will take up much more room on the window-sill or greenhouse staging early in the season. The second reason (perhaps more important) is that you are regularly giving your plants fresh compost through which their roots can move in search of fresh nutrients. If you give the plant all the compost it will eventually need at one go, many of the nutrients will be washed away during watering, before the roots have an opportunity of reaching them. In this case you would have to start 'feeding' the plants at an earlier stage than is usually necessary.

There is extra effort involved, but the results will justify the additional work. Handling your plants regularly is most important, and there is no better way of finding out if anything is wrong than the process of 're-potting'.

The same method of forming a mould in the new container is extremely useful when you come to make up full or half baskets. In this way the positioning of the plants within the container can be seen before the plants are actually placed in the compost.

WATERING

The subject of the frequency and quantity of watering causes anxiety to many gardeners, but there should be no problem provided a few simple rules are remembered.

When preparing the compost for growing fuchsias, it is a good idea to add additional grit or sharp sand to give extra drainage. Fuchsias do not like standing with their roots in a soggy, damp, cold compost, so compost should be moist, as opposed to wet. The rootball should never be allowed to dry out completely, as the roots will shrivel, but if the plant is standing continuously in water the roots will rot and the plant will die.

As to the methods of watering – pouring water on to the top of the compost, or into a saucer, allowing the roots to take up the water they require – either is equally satisfactory. If you water from above (and if your plants are on an indoor window-sill the pots should be standing, to protect the furniture, in a saucer), any excess water that gathers in the saucer should be removed after a few minutes. If you water by filling the saucer in which the plant pot is stand-ing, allow about fifteen minutes for the plant to take up all the moisture it requires and then throw away the excess. Plants growing in a greenhouse may be watered by spraying from

above, an excellent method which also allows the plants to take in moisture through the leaves. The difficulty here is in assessing exactly how much water has been given to each plant. It is better to treat each plant individually, filling the pot to the brim with water and allowing it to drain through the roots and out of the drainage hole in the base of the pot. This method is certainly essential when you are feeding the plants each time you water. Remember – *do not allow your plants to be standing permanently in water*.

It does not seem to matter to any great extent whether water is used directly from the public mains or whether rain water is collected. Regu-larity in applying this moisture is the most im-portant aspect of watering.

You will find that it will not be necessary, in the early part of the year, to water each plant every day, since the lack of warmth in the sun means the extent of evaporation and transpira-tion will not be so great. However, as the season

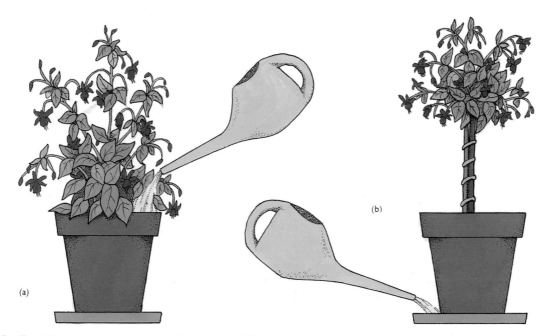

(a)

(b)

Fig 12 *(a) Watering into the compost from above. (b) Watering from below. The water is taken up by capillary action and the excess should be removed after fifteen minutes.*

progresses and the sun rises higher in the sky, it might well be necessary to supply water to your plants once a day, or even more frequently. There can be no rule of thumb laid down, as much will depend upon your own circumstances, but basically the aim will be to maintain a well-drained, moist compost, through which it will be possible to give the essential nutrients to the plants.

In spite of all the gardener's efforts, there are occasions when the compost within the pots completely dries out, perhaps as a result of a weather change during an absence of a couple of days. Unfortunately the peat-based composts are very difficult to re-moisten by normal watering methods, with the water passing straight through the compost and out of the drainage holes. Compost also tends to shrink away from the edge of the pot so that there is an easy exit for the water down the sides. The only real solution to this problem is to immerse the pot and compost completely in a bucket of water, holding it under the water until the bubbles cease rising to the surface. Remove from the bucket and allow to drain, then after a few minutes repeat the process. After the second 'dunking' the compost is usually completely re-moistened. You can now continue watering in the usual way.

Plants growing in hanging baskets, or in patio tubs and in pots standing outside, are open to the elements (the strong sun and drying winds), and will need very careful regular attention. This factor should be taken into consideration in the first instance when you are deciding upon the methods to be used in growing and displaying your plants. When filled with well-grown plants and containing moist compost, a hanging basket will be quite heavy, difficult to move, and might well need watering *in situ*. Accessibility will therefore be an important consideration. Learn to feel the weight of each plant pot, so that you will be able to tell by feel if the plant needs watering. A light weight with light colouring of the surface of the compost will indicate the need for water. A pot which feels heavy, with dark-coloured compost, will probably not. Get to know your plants. A plant which has dull, lifeless-looking leaves which are drooping will probably be suffering from lack of moisture. Conversely (or perhaps perversely), the same symptoms could indicate an excess of moisture and damage to the root system.

If your plant is suffering from excessive watering, and the pot feels very heavy when lifted, drastic treatment will be necessary. Remove the plant from the pot and examine the rootball — if it is very wet, speed up the drying-out process by standing the rootball on an inverted pot and allowing it to drain. If the roots visible around the side of the compost look brown, and perhaps the compost as a whole smells, it might be as well to remove as much of the old compost as possible. This can be done by washing it away under a tap or in a bucket of water. Any damaged and rotting roots should be cut away, and the plant should be re-potted in fresh compost. Treat such plants as invalids for a few days by placing them in a spot shaded from the direct rays of the sun. You should give no additional water to the rootball, but regular spraying overhead will help to refresh the foliage. After a few days, when the foliage is beginning to look perkier, and the roots are obviously beginning to forage in the new compost, the plant can be returned to its normal place on the bench.

FEEDING

During the course of the season you will need to feed your plants. The compost in which you originally placed your fuchsias will, with the passage of time, and with watering, lose its nutritional value. Fuchsias will benefit considerably from regular feeding, and in fact, they are often considered to be gross feeders. All their nutrition is taken up through the roots or through their leaves, so, although it is possible to sprinkle general dry fertilisers around the base of plants, and leave the rain or the water to dissolve the food and take it to the roots, it is easier to supply foods as liquids. The variety of choice available to us these days is immense, but there are basic guidelines as to what a liquid feed should contain.

Any feed should contain nitrogen (N), phosphates (P) and potash (K), together with minute quantities of trace elements such as magnesium, boron, iron, manganese, copper, zinc and molybdenum. On any packet or bottle of fertiliser that you purchase you will see an analysis of the contents. It is the N, P and K numbers which are important, as it is the quantity of each of these elements which will decide when it is best to use the fertiliser.

The 'N' (nitrogen) stimulates the growth of the foliage and helps to build up a good sturdy plant. It is, therefore, essential to have a feed containing a fair proportion of this commodity in the early part of the season when the plant is making good, fast, luscious growth.

The 'P' (phosphate) helps to build up a good strong root system, so, again, this chemical is particularly important at the beginning of the growing cycle of the plant.

The 'K' (potash) is vitally important to plants at all times, as it assists in the use of the nitrogen content of the feed, helps to prevent soft, sappy growth, and helps to improve the colour of the flowers. As the season progresses, potash will help to ripen the wood and prepare the plant for flowering.

The analysis you can expect to find on a packet of feeding crystals will always follow the same layout – three numbers (for example, 25–15–15) will refer to the proportions of nitrogen, phosphates and potash, in that order. Therefore, a feed described as 25–15–15 will have a high nitrogen content, and will be suitable for use at the beginning of the season. A feed with 15–15–30 will have a high potash content, and should be used when the plants have reached the size required and you want to encourage the ripening of the wood and flowering.

As to the frequency of feeding and the strength at which it should be applied, you cannot do better than refer to the label on the packet. Do not be tempted to exceed the recommended dose. Nothing is gained by it and in fact a great deal of harm may be done, as serious scorching and damage of the roots may occur if too great a concentration is used. The recommended strength of feed is one level teaspoon of crystals to each gallon (4.5 litres) of water, applied weekly to your plants. For even better results, try reducing the strength to a quarter and use one level teaspoonful to every 4 gallons (18 litres) of water and apply each time the plant is given a drink. Little and often might be best, and this will also get round the problem of remembering when you last fed your plants.

There are many different types of feed available in garden centres and all are equally useful. Make a habit of examining the labels on the bottles or packets and use the one whose formula is best suited to your needs at that time – high 'N' in the spring, balanced N.P.K. during the main growing season, and high 'K' when flowering is required.

Most of the liquid fertilisers, being very soluble, are also useful for feeding the plant through the leaves (foliar feeding). Although the struc-

Fig 13   Foliar feeding of plants using a hand spray.

21

Fig 15   'Flirtation Waltz', a double-flowered fuchsia.

ture of many leaves prevents a great deal of absorption, this is certainly a valuable means of feeding the plants, especially when they have recently been re-potted and there has been some traumatic disturbance to the root system. Such feeding should only be carried out during the early growing season, and not when young

buds are beginning to form, as it is possible for some marking of the buds and resulting flowers to occur.

Regular feeding of your plants is important and can make all the difference between adequate plants and those of which you can be proud.

Fig 14   (Preceding page) 'Brutus'.

CHAPTER 3

Increasing your Stock

CUTTINGS

One of the best things about growing fuchsias is the opportunity you have of increasing the number of your plants by taking cuttings. Many, perhaps most, plants can be reproduced by taking cuttings. Some are extremely difficult and need ideal conditions, whereas others will root very readily. Fuchsias come into the second category, and you will find that it is the simplest of operations to persuade a piece of a fuchsia plant to root. I once attended a meeting where the speaker was discussing the methods by which another genus could be persuaded to root; he suddenly threw in the comment, 'Of course you fuchsia growers are lucky; you only have to drop a cutting on a damp floor and it will root!' Perhaps an exaggeration, but certainly close to the truth.

Various things are needed for success in rooting cuttings. First and foremost you will require good stock material. Secondly, you need a propagator and compost, and moistness and warmth, not heat – I am sure that the vast majority of failures that occur are as a result of excessive heat. If you provide good, warm, humid conditions for your young cuttings, they will root in about two to three weeks.

Compost

How do you go about it? First, you need to consider the compost in which cuttings will root. Fuchsia cuttings will in fact root in pure water, as well as moist sand, vermiculite, perlite, or any other substance which will retain moisture. They will therefore root easily in pure peat. You may

have been advised that the compost in which the cuttings are initially rooted should contain no nutrient at all. In fact, a mixture of 50 per cent peat and 50 per cent sharp sand, vermiculite or perlite, is often recommended by leading growers and nurserymen. This excellent material will hold moisture, and, with the addition of warmth, roots can be encouraged to form. With that warmth, following the rules of nature, those roots will immediately start foraging for food. If the compost contains no food, the plant, in its anxiety to find nutrients, will form more and more roots to join the frantic search. An excellent root system is therefore built up very quickly. When it has developed sufficiently, and is transferred into a compost containing the essential foods, it will help to build up an excellent plant. For this to work, you must be in the position to pot on your cuttings at the correct time. Failure to do so will result in stunted and woody growth, since you will not have provided the young rooted cutting with the essential nutrients.

I prefer a compost consisting of a mixture of my normal potting compost, with an equal portion of vermiculite. Adding vermiculite reduces the nutritional value of the compost (although there is some present). When they are inserted in this compost and given moisture and warmth, the cuttings root and when they start foraging for food they are successful in finding it. As a result the roots develop, and the plant will start to grow and will remain succulent. The resulting root system might not be as extensive as that developed in pure peat, but it will, nevertheless, be quite adequate.

Containers

The second thing to consider is the type of container in which to root your cuttings. You need something in which a high humidity can be maintained, as you must be sure that, once you have severed the cutting from the parent plant, there will be no wilting or loss of moisture from that cutting before the roots have formed. There are many types of containers available, but you may well find that the cheapest are the most effective.

At the top of the price range are electrically-heated propagators, which are the size of one or two seed trays and have a perspex cover. These are excellent and can be used not only for rooting your fuchsia cuttings, but also for germinating some of those more difficult seeds which require higher tempratures. The one fault with this type of propagator is that they are *too* good, and give too much heat for the successful rooting of fuchsia cuttings. However, you can reduce the heat, so that you have a gentle warmth, by placing a layer of gravel, sand or perlite in the base of the tray. This insulation will also be a means by which a high humidity can be maintained.

Another simple propagator that can be purchased at a reasonable price is a half or full tray unheated propagator, again with a perspex dome. These are excellent as they can be used on a window-sill, and the heat of the room is

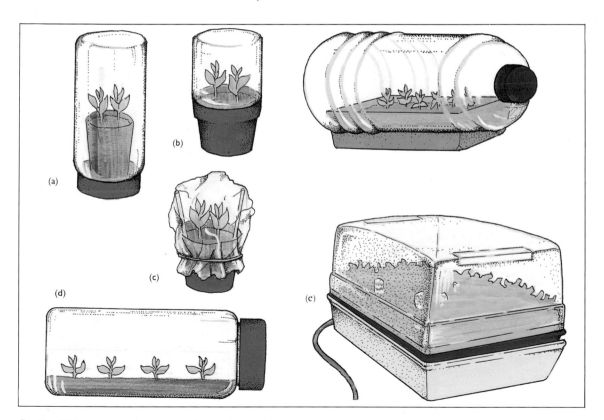

Fig 16   *Different types of propagator that can be used: (a) an inverted coffee jar; (b) a jam jar inverted on a pot; (c) a plastic bag covering a pot, held away from the cuttings by small sticks and secured by an elastic band; (d) a plastic sweet jar on its side, with the lid kept on to maintain humidity; (e) an electric seed tray sized propagator.*

sufficient to assist the rooting process. Within a half tray sized propagator it is possible to root a considerable number of cuttings at one go, depending upon the size of the cuttings that you take.

As you are looking for some structure which will maintain a humid atmosphere around the cuttings, it is possible, with imagination, to think of many useful, and free, types of propagator covers. If you invert a large coffee jar, and stand a small flower pot on the lid, you have the perfect propagator. A large jam jar, again inverted and covering a 3½in (9cm) pot can also be used. Other examples are cut-down plastic lemonade bottles, plastic sweet jars, and plastic bags supported by wires or sticks.

Preparation

When taking a cutting, you are looking for a piece of the plant which you can remove from the parent plant and encourage to root, and it is possible that some pieces will root more easily than others. Given the right conditions, practially any part of the fuchsia plant will form roots, but it is useful to know which parts are most likely to be successful, and which will root the easiest. Without doubt the best cutting material is found at the ends of young shoots. The very end tip of each shoot is referred to as the soft green tip, and in the early part of the year such shoots are easily obtained. For details of the parts most suitable for use as cuttings see the diagram below.

Before preparing the cutting for insertion into the cutting compost you must have everything ready. Above all, it is important that the cutting, once severed from the parent plant, should not be allowed to wilt. Prepare the compost by placing it in the container and giving it a watering using a fine rose on a watering can. The cuttings can now be prepared. The usual recommendation is that a cutting is removed from the parent by cutting just beneath a leaf node (see Fig 17).

Fig 17   A number of cuttings are available from one branch of a fuchsia plant.

Fig 18   'Swingtime'.

The bottom leaves are then removed, and ideally you will be left with a cutting about 2in (5cm) long with a growing tip and two pairs of young leaves. Given the right conditions, such a cutting will root well. However, it is not necessary to remove from the plant by cutting below the leaf node – this also removes the small embryo shoots situated in the leaf axils which, if left, will develop into new shoots. I remove a piece of plant by cutting just *above* the leaf node; the length of my cutting will be about 1–1½in (2.5–4cm) and it will consist of a growing tip and one set of leaves.

Having prepared your cutting in either way, gently push it into the compost. If a number of cuttings are placed in the same container, you should water them in, again using a very fine rose

on a watering can. This will have the effect of settling the compost around the cuttings. A label bearing the name of the plant from which the cuttings were taken, together with the date upon which the operation was carried out, is inserted, and the whole is covered with its propagator cover.

Conditions and Care

It is now a matter of time before our cuttings will form roots but we must ensure that they are given the right conditions. The propagator can be placed on a window-sill in the house, where the ambient temperature will be sufficient to assist in the formation of roots. Do not, however, place the propagator on a window-sill which is facing towards the sun, as the warmth of the sun shining through the window and the cover of the propagator will create considerable heat, and the cuttings will be killed. A north-facing window is ideal. If you have to use a south-facing one, you will have to provide some form of shading from the sun.

It will also be necessary to provide some shading in the confines of a greenhouse.

The cuttings should be prevented from wilting at all costs, being looked at daily and, if necessary, being given a spray with fresh water. Cuttings in coffee jars will not need this attention, as the moisture within the pot is unable to escape. For the best possible success in rooting, you should aim for a temperature of approximately 60°F (15–16°C).

Within ten to fourteen days indications should appear to tell you that the cuttings are beginning to form their roots. Shortly after the cuttings are removed from the parent plants they will take on a rather dull look, but when rooting commences a healthy, glossy look appears and the cuttings begin to look more sprightly. At this stage the cuttings should be left in their ideal situations for another week so that all the cuttings in the container have the opportunity of forming roots. To prevent any shock to the young plants, it is advisable to wean them away gently from their humid environment. Raise the edge of the propagator top for a short time during the first two days to allow fresh air to pass among the cuttings. Gradually increase the amount of air allowed to the plants until, by the end of the week, the propagator top can be completely removed from its position, and the young plants will be able to survive quite happily.

The cuttings can remain in their containers for a further week before it will be necessary to consider placing them in their individual pots. If the compost in which you rooted your cuttings contained no nutrients (perhaps a 50/50 mixture of peat and perlite), it will be necessary to add some food to the compost by watering with a dilute liquid feed. I would suggest a high nitrogen feed, diluted to a quarter of the normal recom-

mended strength (1 level teaspoon to four gallons (18 litres) of water). If your compost contained some nutrient there will be no need to start feeding until the first potting has taken place.

Cuttings may be taken at any time of the year, provided the correct amount of warmth can be given. If you wish to obtain good-sized plants for flowering in early to late summer, then the earlier the cuttings are rooted the better. Cuttings rooted in February will grow into plants large enough to be placed and flower in 5–6in (13–15cm) pots by July. Cuttings may be taken (as an insurance policy), in late summer or early autumn, from plants growing in the garden which will be left in that situation. Over-wintering young green tip cuttings inside your house will ensure that, should a very severe frost cause the demise of any plant in the open garden, you will have a new, young plant ready to replace it in the spring.

OTHER CUTTINGS

Many growers of the superb plants exhibited on show benches prefer to grow their fuchsias using the 'biennial' method. That is, they will grow their plants to a certain size in the first year and will allow them to flower the following year, having trained them into very bushy plants or standards. Cuttings for this type of growth are usually taken in May and June when no artificial warmth will be necessary, and the young plants are allowed to develop into bushy shapes by continual 'stopping' of the growing tips. Such plants do not have a winter's rest but are encouraged to stay in green leaf through the winter months, being kept at sufficient temperature to ensure they remain alive.

It is possible to take harder wood cuttings of plants in the late autumn, and these can be

Fig 19 (Opposite) Fuchsias grown in a mixed border.

28

rooted by being left in a cold frame throughout the winter. This is not a particularly satisfactory method, but it is the means by which plants can be grown to be used later as hedges.

Green tip cuttings are not the only type of cuttings that will root easily. Although they are perhaps the simplest of all, it is fair to say that practically any part of a fuchsia plant can be encouraged to root. Should it be your good fortune to find a branch of one of your plants 'sporting' a flower or leaves of a different colour, you will want to obtain as many cuttings as possible from that branch. The soft green tip will supply just one. However, if you look down the stem you will see that there are small shoots appearing at each leaf axil, and these can be used quite satisfactorily. A piece of stem containing leaves can be cut both above and below the leaves and this will provide another cutting. If the shoots further down the branch are slightly longer, it is possible to remove the part containing the leaves and, by carefully slicing down through the piece of stem, two small cuttings will

be available. For the type of cuttings that can be obtained and the number that it is possible to root from just one stem, see the diagram on page 26 of a fuchsia stem.

The secret of success in the rooting of cuttings is to maintain a humid atmosphere around the young cutting so that it does not lose its turgidity by too great a transpiration. If the base of the cutting material is kept moist and the leaves do not flag, then rooting will certainly take place.

CROSSING

When talking about propagation you automatically think of taking cuttings from a plant and encouraging rooting – propagation can really be defined as increasing by natural process, and there are other means by which you can increase the number of your fuchsias. Taking cuttings (removing a piece of a parent plant) will give you, when it is rooted, an exact copy of the original plant – a cutting from 'Border Queen'

Fig 20   Using an egg box as a propagator.

Fig 21 Fuchsia fulgens.

will become a plant of 'Border Queen'. This means that you are able easily to increase the amount of stock you hold of any one type of plant. However, it does not enable you to produce new types of plants – new cultivars. The taking of a cutting from a plant is known as 'vegetative reproduction', while the way in which new cultivars can be obtained, by the crossing of one cultivar with another, is known as 'sexual reproduction'. The resultant seed obtained from such crossings will produce a new plant which bears the characteristics of each of its parents, and is different from its seed-bearing parent.

New cultivars can be easily obtained, as is shown by the vast number (some ten thousand) which are available today. Unfortunately many of the 'new' cultivars are very similar to those already obtainable, and are no improvement upon them. The work of the hybridiser should

always be to improve what is already obtainable, in terms of resistance to disease, strength of stem, greater flowering potential, colour, and so on. It is important therefore that any prospective plant breeder should have the strength of character to be selective. A ripe berry from a fuchsia plant may produce scores of seeds, all of which, if given the right conditions, will germinate and grow into flowering plants. Many of these will be inferior plants with many weaknesses, others will be very similar to other cultivars, and very few will show an improvement upon what has gone before. The breeder should, as soon as the type of growth and flower is known, sort out those which are worthy of further consideration, and then dispose of the rest. A really dedicated breeder will save perhaps a dozen from a thousand or more seedlings. Strength of character is certainly necessary.

Fig 22 'Swingtime'.

The methods by which the pollen of one plant is transferred to another plant for fertilisation to take place are discussed fully in other publications, and the grower who is anxious to try his hand at hybridising will need to make a study of the subject in order to formulate a programme of research and improvement. Each hybridiser needs to have an aim and should have a mental picture of the type of plant he or she is attempting to produce.

SEEDS

It is possible to obtain packets of fuchsia seeds which, when grown, will produce new plants. As already stated, plants resulting from the sowing of such seed will be new cultivars and might well be extremely disappointing. Conversely, it is possible that one excellent new cultivar might be found which will be a complete breakthrough from anything that has gone before. One of the problems about buying packets of seed concerns the percentage of germination that you should be prepared to accept. For the best possible results, seeds from the fuchsia should be sown as soon as possible after removal from the berry. There will inevitably be a long delay from harvesting to sowing when seeds are purchased. An ordinary seed sowing compost is suitable, and it is recommended that the seed should not be buried but lightly pressed into the surface of the compost. The compost should be kept moist by watering from below or very gently spraying from above. If a temperature of 65–70°F (18–21°C) can be maintained, germination should occur fairly quickly. When the seedlings are large enough to handle they should be pricked out into individual small pots and then grown on in the same way as small rooted cuttings. Beware of damping off disease brought about by a lack of ventilation.

Do not be in a hurry to throw away the compost in which your seedlings were germinated, as it is possible that other seedlings will appear later. It is worth waiting for these, as it is often the case that those seeds which have been slower to germinate produce the nicest plants.

SPORTING

The production and the sowing of seeds is not the only method by which new varieties can be produced. Occasionally, plants produce a shoot which has flowers or leaves of a different colour or shape – this is known as 'sporting'. It is surprising how plants of the same cultivar, in vastly differing parts of the country, will in the same season start producing such branches. (Unfortunately, this multi-production of 'sports' usually means that different names are given to the same type of plant by the growers.) The finding of branches which are different from the parent plant is a matter of observation. Growers who are really looking after their plants and handling them daily are far more likely to notice

Fig 23   'Annabel' in a window box.

the variation in colour of a flower or leaf. If you find such a 'sport', it will be important for you to secure new plants from the varying branch. To secure the new variety you just need to take cuttings from that branch, and such cuttings will hopefully reproduce the new colouring. You will probably have to grow such new plants for two or three years, to ensure that the new colouring has been fixed and that the plant does not revert to the colouring of its parent.

When you produce a new cultivar, whether it is by growing a new seedling or by securing a 'sport', it is advisable to ask the advice of other enthusiastic growers of fuchsias as to the relative merits of your new 'baby'. If the response obtained is favourable, you should grow the new plant to its full potential, in as many differing shapes as possible, and put it forward for public examination on the show bench at a specialist fuchsia show. The judges will be able to advise you on the future prospects of your plants. If you have been extremely lucky and have produced a potential winner, a specialist fuchsia nurseryman will certainly be interested in discussing your plant with you. No fortunes have ever been made in producing new fuchsias, but there is considerable satisfaction in seeing the name of your introduction appearing among the winners at national shows.

The naming of fuchsias is very much a personal matter, but you should bear in mind that names which are already in use should not be given to a new plant. There is an International Registrar based in America for the registration of fuchsia names but there is, unfortunately, no

Fig 25   'Vera Wolyn' sport.

legal requirement that names should be registered. The International Registrar of Fuchsias can be contacted at The American Fuchsia Society, Hall of Flowers, Garden Centre of San Francisco, 9th Avenue and Lincoln Way, San Francisco, California 94122, USA.

Fig 24   (Preceding page) 'Celia Smedley'.

CHAPTER 4

Shaping your Plants

When your cuttings are well rooted and beginning to grow you will need to consider for what purpose you intend to use them. If you just leave them now, they will continue to grow straight up the central stem, wandering around rather like a vine, and will soon be out of control. Also, the number of flowers is determined by the number of branches or 'laterals' on the plant, so you need to encourage your fuchsias to produce as many branches as possible (unless you want to grow a standard or tree fuchsia).

STOPPING

Generally, people want good bushy plants, but the natural desire of most fuchsias is to grow straight along the central stem. For this reason you need to encourage side shoots to form, in order to prevent that upward growth. When your rooted cutting has produced three or four sets of leaves, you can remove the small growing tip from the centre of the plant. The smallest piece possible should be removed – bend the small tip at right angles to the first pair of leaves, and it will snap off very easily without damage to any of the small shoot buds that may be in the leaf axils. Some growers remove the small tip by using scissors or razor blades, while others resort to finger and thumb nails – each of these methods is dangerous for those small developing shoots. Provided the young plants have been well watered and are quite turgid, bending the growing tip over at right angles to the next pair of leaves will snap it off cleanly without the young shoots being touched.

The result of this 'stopping' of the plant is that

those young shoots in the leaf axils will receive all the nutrient that would have made its way to the leading growing tip, and each will now start to develop and grow into a new young branch. Where you had one growing tip (if there were three pairs of leaves on the plant when you

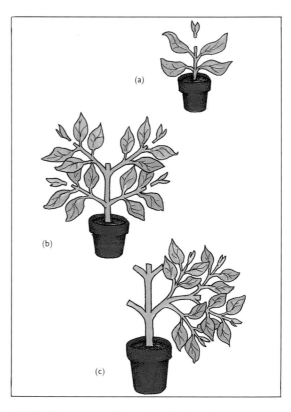

Fig 26 The process of 'stopping' a fuchsia plant in three stages: (a) remove the smallest growing tip; (b) remove the growing tips from the resultant growth; (c) four new shoots should grow from the leaf axils on each of the four branches.

'stopped' it), you now have six – six new branches which will produce for you six times the quantity of flowers. If you allow these six branches to develop until they have each produced two or three pairs of leaves, you can then remove the growing tip from each of them, and this will mean that on each branch four or six new branches should grow. If you multiply this by the six branches you will see that you now have a nice bushy plant, with either twenty-four or thirty-six branches, and you will not have to do any further 'stopping' of your plants.

If you wish, you can continue the process each time the new shoots produce two pairs of leaves, and your plants will become bigger and bushier. However, you must remember that the action of stopping the growth encourages the production of new branches, and will delay the production of flower buds. The buds are formed in the very tips of each branch, so the removal of those tips delays flowering until new ones have been grown. As a rough guide, if the flowers from your plant are usually single (four petals only), then there will be a delay of approximately eight weeks before flowers appear. If your plant produces double flowers (five or more petals in the corolla), an additional two weeks must be allowed before the flowers can be expected.

The earlier in the season you can start your training of the plants, the bigger they can be-

Fig 27   Stages of growth and subsequent stopping.

come and the more flowers they will bear. Generally, for the purpose of outdoor displays, just two 'stoppings' will be sufficient to give some excellent plants. Those gardeners growing for show or exhibition purposes will undoubtedly require a greater number of 'breaks'.

If you wish to produce plants suitable for use in baskets (usually plants which have shown a rather lax type of growth, which will cascade down over the edge of the basket), the type of training described above is all that you need. The young plants can be 'stopped' at three pairs of leaves and then 'stopped' for a second time when a further three pairs of leaves have been formed. This will give you nice bushy plants which can be placed around your basket, and will give you an excellent show over a long period of time. Plants for planting out permanently in the garden can also be produced in the same way.

If you wish to grow your cuttings into shapes other than bushes or shrubs, a different method of training will need to be adopted.

STANDARDS

I have often heard standard fuchsias called tree fuchsias – a very fair description of them, since what they are is a bush fuchsia growing on a stem. First, you have to grow the stem.

The natural desire of the fuchsia is to grow straight along the first stem, with all its strength and vigour being concentrated on that central growing tip. Select a good, strong cutting, preferably one with leaves growing in threes along the stem as opposed to the usual twos, place a flower stick alongside the cutting and gently secure the stem to it with soft twine. This will serve two purposes – it will remind you that this cutting is to be grown on as a standard, and should not therefore have its central tip removed, and also it will encourage the stem to grow straight. Ensure that you secure the stem to the cane loosely as it will thicken as it grows, and you do not want to make an indentation into

Fig 28 'Michelle Wallace', a sport from 'Countess of Aberdeen'.

the plant should be re-potted into the next size of pot and given fresh compost. This new compost will encourage fresh root growth and with that extra root growth will come faster top growth. Failure to pot on into larger pots with fresh compost will cause the plant to become 'pot-bound'. Because of the lack of nutrients available to the roots (even if copious supplies of liquid fertiliser are being fed into the pot), the plant will feel threatened. Its reaction will be to produce its flowers, so that seed will be set and the species continued. When the upward-growing standard feels threatened, the flower buds will be formed and upward growth will cease. This is not what you want, so you must do all you can to ensure the continued vegetative growth of your plant. Regular re-potting will provide the additional nutrients and the root space for continued growth, both below and above the surface of the compost.

Fig 29 'Sheila Hobson'.

the stem nor prevent the passage of nutrients up its length. As the plant develops it is possible that young shoots will appear in the leaf axils up the stem. As these will rob the main growing tip of some of its vigour, it is advisable gently to remove these young shoots as they form. This can be done by bending them at right angles to the stem and so snapping them off cleanly. If they are left until they are much bigger, and then removed with a knife, a scar may result – this will be disfiguring when the plant is mature.

The stem will grow upwards at quite a speed and attention should be paid to the pot in which it is growing. At regular intervals the plant should be removed from the pot and the rootball examined. When a good number of roots are showing on the outside of the compost, and before they have time to start encircling the pot,

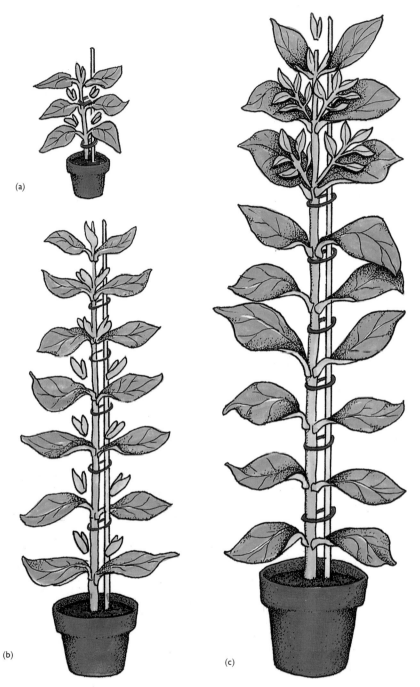

Fig 30   The development of a 'standard': (a) remove all side shoots from leaf
axils; (b) leave all leaves, but remove lower side shoots, and then leave top three
sets of side shoots as the stem develops; (c) remove growing tip and allow three
sets of shoots to develop into the head.

39

Fig 31   The potting on of a growing standard from a smaller pot into a larger one, using the mould-forming method.

It is possible that by the time the plant has reached the height you require (and this can be anything up to about 4ft (120cm)), your plant will have been moved from a 2in (5cm) to a 7in (17.5cm) pot, in 1in (2.5cm) stages.

When the 'whip' (the name for a cutting being grown as a standard) has grown to about 12in (30cm) in height, you can leave the top three sets of shoots in the leaf axils as they develop. As a further set develops at the top of the plant, the lower set can be removed, so that you always have three sets of shoots available to form a head in case anything should happen to the growing tip.

When the whip reaches the height you require, having three sets of shoots in the top three sets of leaf axils, the process of forming the bush on the top of your stem can commence. Remove the growing tip. This will now encourage all the strength and vigour of the plant to go into those three sets of shoots which you have left on the plant. They will grow, and when they have each formed two sets of leaves, their growing tips can be removed. Your six (or nine) branches in the head can now be multiplied by four. This could be sufficient in the first season, and you can then allow each of these branches to develop and produce their flowers. If you have enough patience you can, when two pairs of leaves have grown on each of your branches, remove the growing tips to quadruple the number of branches again.

Fig 32 '*Torville and Dean*', *a double-flowered fuchsia.*

Fig 33 'Cotton Candy'.

The eventual height your standard reaches will depend upon your own wishes. However, if at some future date you are so pleased with your standard fuchsia that you would like to enter it in a show, you will need to know the measurements required by the show schedule. A miniature standard is one growing in a 5in (13cm) pot, with a clear stem not in excess of 10in (25cm) – a clear stem is measured from the level of the compost to the first branch. A quarter standard is one on which the stem is no less than 10in (25cm), nor more than 18in (45cm). A half standard has a clear stem of between 18in (45cm) and 30in (75cm). A full standard commences at 30in (75cm), and does not exceed 42in (105cm). Usually in the case of the quarter, half and full standards, the size of the pot is irrelevant, although it ought to be in proportion to the plant.

Standard fuchsias are ideal subjects for planting out in the garden during the summer as 'dot' plants. They give that very important extra height to any flower bed, and are always a very good focus and talking point. One word of warning – even if the cultivar you have used to grow your standard is considered a 'hardy' variety, it should not be left in the garden over winter, as the very first severe frost will kill the stem. As it takes at least six months to grow this stem it would be a pity to lose it. Standards do need extra protection during the winter (see Chapter 6).

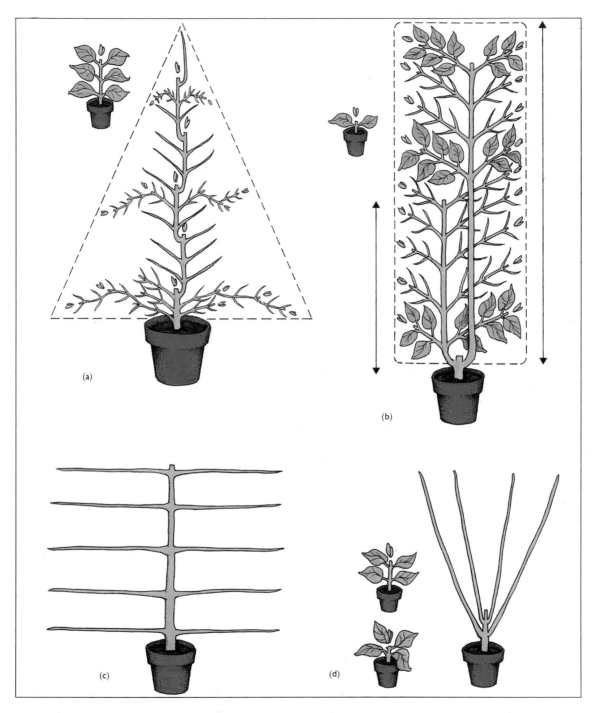

*Fig 34   Methods of training. (a) For a pyramid shape; (b) for a pillar formation;
(c) for an espalier; (d) for either a three-stemmed or a four-stemmed fan.*

43

Fig 35 *'Joy Patmore'.*

These paragraphs cover only the simplest forms of training, and there are others which I would suggest are worth trying when you have gained greater expertise in the growing of these plants. It is possible to grow fuchsias as pillars, pyramids, fans and espaliers, but it will be important to have sufficient space available for the over-wintering and growing of these larger speci-mens. They are extremely time-consuming and, as they can be growing and flowering for you over a period of eight or more years, they can become very much a part of the family and somewhat of a liability when holidays, and so on, are being planned! At the other end of the spectrum it is also possible to train fuchsias in miniature, as bonsai trees.

CHAPTER 5

Displaying Fuchsias

FUCHSIAS IN THE GARDEN

Fuchsias will combine with practically any other type of flower to make an extremely good show in the garden. There are really two ways in which one can approach the use of fuchsias in the garden: as half-hardy annuals used as temporary bedding subjects, or as permanent bedding plants. (They can also be used as hedging, but really the permanent bedding and hedging can be treated as one.)

Bearing in mind that fuchsias are frost-shy plants, the initial planting of either temporary or permanent bedding schemes should be left until all risk of frost has passed – usually not until the beginning of June. It should also be borne in mind that when planting in a permanent border great care needs to be taken over the preparation of the site, as the plants, once established, will remain in the same position for many years. The ground will need to be well dug, and a quantity of fertiliser should be added for a good food supply for the foraging roots. It is beneficial to dig in quantities of peat so that the earth surrounding the plants remains moist.

As with all bedding schemes, far greater impact is made on the eye if a group of plants of the same cultivar are planted together, perhaps in groups of three or five. Care should also be taken to ensure that the plants used will grow to a reasonable height, with those expected to reach the greatest height at the back of the

Fig 36   Simple plan for the layout of a fuchsia bed, with the low-growing 'Thumb' family in the front and standards in the centre.

Fig 37   Fuchsias in a border.

border. On a temporary basis, quarter, half or full standards are extremely useful to give that all-important height. Under no circumstances should plants trained as standards be allowed to remain in the garden when frosts threaten. The first severe frost will kill off the stem and all the time and trouble taken to grow it will have been wasted.

Strong, upright-growing plants should be chosen, preferably those which hold their flowers in the semi-horizontal or upright positions. For temporary use it is not necessary to confine yourself to those plants which are considered to be hardy (that is, capable of remaining in the same position throughout the winter and sending up fresh young shoots the following spring). You can therefore choose any from the long lists of plants now available. When choosing your colour scheme it might be as well to

consider the colouring of the leaves. Plants of the *Triphylla* type with their dark green leaves and purple underleaf are extremely attractive, even while you are awaiting the arrival of the flowers. There are other variegated and yellow-leaved varieties which are equally useful.

When planting your border you should space your plants, which hopefully will be growing in 3½in (9cm) or 5in (13cm) pots, at a distance of 15–18in (37.5–45cm) apart. For those which will be remaining in the site permanently, the method of planting will make a considerable difference to their hardiness. After the first severe frosts in the autumn, the plants will be denuded of leaves and the protection of the rootball will be your primary consideration. You will need to give each rootball some protection or insulation from deep frosts, as it is from the rootball that you hope new shoots will grow in the following spring. To give this extra protection from severe frosts it is advisable to plant your fuchsias deeper than is normally recommended for other flowering shrubs. The usual recommendation is to plant at the same level in the ground as the surface of the compost in the pot. However, although this will give some protection, the top of the rootball will be very near the surface of the soil. You should really aim to get that rootball about 2in (5cm) lower than the soil surface, and one of the easiest ways of doing this, without immediately covering some of the lower branches and leaves with soil, is to prepare a saucer-shaped indentation in the ground, about 2in (5cm) deep in the centre, for each plant. At the centre of each saucer the fuchsia can be planted so that its compost level is the same as the lower level of the soil. During the course of the summer, with the watering and cultivating around the plants, the saucer shape will be filled in and the rootball will be a couple of inches lower than the normal soil level. This means important extra insulation.

Do not be tempted to remove the branches from your permanent bedding plants when the first frosts have removed the leaves. Leave them on the plants until the spring, as they will give added protection from the severe frosts and will also indicate the position of each plant. In the spring, when fresh growth is being produced from below the surface of the soil, you can cut away the old branches to make room for the new flowering branches that will grow.

Although your fuchsias have been planted in a well-cultivated piece of ground, it is unwise to assume that they can now be left to fend for themselves. They will need the same sort of treatment that you give to plants growing in pots. Watering will need to be carried out, especially at the beginning of the season as the plants become established, and also in those long, dry, sunny spells we all dream about. Regular feeding will pay dividends as it will encourage fresh young growth and a multitude of flowers. Keep an eye open also for pests and diseases. In the open the capsid bug is a bit of a

Fig 38   Planting in the garden using a saucer-shaped indentation so that the plant is inserted at the correct level.

47

problem, as it bites the succulent young tip of the shoots, causing loss of flowering. A regular spraying with a systemic insecticide will keep your plants clear. White fly is less of a problem in the open, but it is something that does need to be watched for.

As the flowering season draws to a close you may become worried about the possibility of your plants not surviving the winter. If so, there is nothing to stop you from lifting some of the plants, cleaning them and storing them in pots or boxes in a frost-free place. However, it is better to leave your plants in the garden, giving them a little extra protection with peat, bracken or other insulating material. Also, you could take some pre-winter cuttings in case of disaster. You may have noticed in the heavy misty mornings of autumn that the fuchsias seem to take on a new lease of life. Fresh, young, green growth appears on the ends of most branches as the plants experience the type of humid, moist conditions which they enjoy so much in their native habitat. Small pieces of these new shoots can be removed from the plants as green tip cuttings. If placed in a propagator they will root quite readily with no additional warmth, and can be

nurtured through the winter with very little difficulty. At this stage of the season there is no rush for root formation, so a simple unheated propagator in a cool place will be ideal. Rooting could take up to four weeks in such conditions, and the resultant plants can be allowed to remain within the propagators in a frost-free place, growing slowly as the winter months progress. If the rooted cuttings start to outgrow their containers, perhaps in late November or December, then the process can be repeated, the tips of each rooted cutting being used to make fresh soft green tip cutting material. By the time the fresh young cuttings have rooted and are growing well, spring will be just around the corner and a supply of bedding plants will be ready, just in case your outdoor plants have succumbed to the wintry weather.

Recommended Cultivars for the Garden

Alice Hoffman, Brutus, Charming, Display, Dorothy, Empress of Prussia, Garden News, Genii, Herald, Lady Thumb, Margaret, Margaret Brown, Pixie, Rufus (the Red), Snowcap, Son of Thumb, Tennessee Waltz, and Tom Thumb.

This is a very brief list of suitable cultivars for permanently bedding outside, and a glance through any nurseryman's catalogue will give names of many others. Within these catalogues you will often see the codes 'H1', 'H2', and 'H3'. These codes can be defined as follows:

H1 requires a greenhouse heated to a minimum of 40°F (4 to 5°C)
H2 requires cool greenhouse – half-hardy
H3 denotes that the plant is considered hardy

FUCHSIAS ON THE PATIO

There is no better way to show off your fuchsias than by growing them out of doors and it does not really matter whether you have a large

Fig 39   A coffee jar propagator.

Fig 40   A patio decorated with fuchsias.

Fig 41   Fuchsias decorating a garage.

Fig 42　'Jack Shahan' grown in a bottle.

garden or just a small area – the fuchsia will enhance your surroundings and will be a focal point around which other plants can grow. On the patio, you will be growing your plants in what might be considered to be unnatural conditions (within confined root spaces). However, growing plants in tubs or baskets is no different from growing plants in pots in the greenhouse, and as such is quite possible.

There are various containers that are available for use, but your immediate instinct might be to raise the plants away from the ground, where they can be viewed from their best possible angle. Looking up into the pendulous flowers is the way to admire their shape and form. Suspending plants growing in hanging baskets or pots is therefore most important, and baskets can be successfully fixed to the walls so that flowers can cascade down. If there is insufficient room for full-sized baskets it might well be possible to suspend hanging pots. At ground level, troughs of various shapes and sizes

can be used, as can large ornamental urns. Window-sills make ideal resting places for narrow troughs where plants can be appreciated from both inside and outside the house. You do not need to confine yourself to the type of container that can be purchased, however. There is a great deal of satisfaction in being able to manufacture suitable containers yourself, or recycling objects made for another purpose.

Although some enthusiasts of the fuchsia would prefer to see their favourite plants growing in isolation, I feel that fuchsias grown in co-ordination with other types of annuals, hardy or half-hardy, will produce a beautiful display.

It is important when considering these outdoor displays to remember that you are dealing with frost-tender plants, and that it would be unwise to place them in their final flowering positions until all risks of frost have passed – not until the first of June. Even after that date, you should keep an eye on the weather forecast and, should a frost warning be given, take the necessary and simple protective actions.

Any type of fuchsia will be suitable for use in the patio garden. Plants for the hanging pots and baskets need to be of the laxer pendulous type, but upright growers of all shapes and hues will be suitable for ground containers.

Baskets

It is always a good idea for a basket of fuchsias to contain a number of plants of the same cultivar. If a variety of cultivars is used you will find that their rate of growth and time of flowering will vary. A basket completely covered with foliage and flowers is a marvellous sight, and it should look the same, whichever angle it is viewed from. The number of plants you require for each basket will depend upon its diameter – a basket with a diameter of 12in (30cm) will need four plants of a strong growing cultivar (three around the edges and one in the centre); a 15in (37.5cm) basket will need five. Most basket varieties are strong vigorous growers but some, especially those with smaller leaves and small flowers, will

Fig 43   A fuchsia display in a tub.

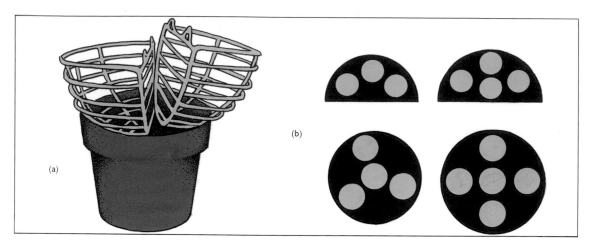

Fig 44 (a) Supporting wire half baskets while planting. (b) Positions for planting in half and full baskets.

require additional plants, so that the basket is a complete ball of flower.

Although the basket will not be placed in its final position (from a bracket attached to the house, or on a pedestal) until June, it is advisable to make arrangements for the basket to be planted with well-grown plants and to be kept growing strongly in a warm environment ahead of this date. The best basket plants will be those grown from cuttings taken very early in the year, or even during the previous autumn. Preferably they will be growing in 3½in (9cm) pots and will have good, well-branched growth. The wire hemispherical-shaped baskets are perhaps the most popular, and should be planted as follows.

The shape (rounded bottom) of the basket will make it difficult to keep the container still during the planting operation – try placing the basket in a large flower pot, tub or bucket. The first requirement will be some substance to prevent the compost from falling through the gaps in the wire. Many growers use moss for this purpose, but I prefer to use a sheet of plastic, preferably black, cut to size. Drainage holes need to be made in this plastic sheet so that excess water can escape. The compost should be a peat-based one, as the weight of a basket filled with a loam-based compost is too great.

Place the liner in the basket and add three or four handfuls of a just moist compost, to give you a layer of about 2in (5cm) in the base of the

basket. Take pots of the same size as those in which your plants are growing and place them in position on the compost. Some growers recommend that the outer pots should be placed at a slight angle to encourage the trailing over of the plants, but this is not necessary. Once the pots are positioned, pour compost into each one until they are overflowing, and continue until the

Fig 45 Making a hanging basket, supporting the wire container on a large pot.

52

Fig 46   *A fuchsia display in Lechlade nursery, Gloucestershire.*

basket is completely full of compost. The rims of the pots should be just visible and the compost surrounding them can be settled by gently bouncing the basket on its base. Remove the pot from the centre of the basket, leaving a moulded indentation the exact size of the pots from which you will be taking your plants. Remove one plant from the pot in which it was growing by inverting it, and place it in the moulded hole – it will, of course, fit perfectly. The same process is adopted for each of the other plants, dealing with them one at a time. When the last plant is in position the whole basket can be given a good watering to further settle the compost around the plants, using a fine rose on a watering can. The basket is now complete and, if it has been made up prior to the recommended date for planting outside, it can be allowed to grow and become fully established within the greenhouse.

Once the basket is hanging in its flowering position it will need to be tended very carefully.

Baskets are open to the drying elements of the wind and the sun, and will therefore need watering daily – perhaps even twice a day in the height of the summer. Care must therefore be taken to ensure that they are easily accessible and that a supply of water is to hand. As flowers are produced and then die, it is important to ensure that seed pods are removed in order to maintain a constant supply of flowers through-out the season – once the plant's task of produc-ing seeds has been performed, flowering will slow down and perhaps even stop. It will also be necessary to feed the plants during the season to maintain their vigour – high nitrogen feed in the early part of the season, balanced feed during the summer months, and a high potash feed later. Try to get into a habit of feeding your plants on a regular basis so that there is no possibility of this task being forgotten. Whilst feeding or watering, keep a wary eye open for any pests that may be around. Plants growing

Fig 47   Fuchsias around a pond.

54

out of doors seem to suffer far less than their indoor compatriots, but nevertheless they are very popular with both greenfly and white fly. A regular spraying programme to prevent the build-up of any of these pests is advisable.

Half baskets, or 'wall baskets' as they are sometimes called, are dealt with in a similar way. A basket with a width of 12in (30cm) should hold four plants, three around the front edge and one central. Perhaps the easiest way to keep these baskets still while working on them is to place two back to back within a large pot, tub or bucket. Fixing these baskets to the wall is a relatively easy task, but you must make sure that the rear of the basket is parallel to the wall, so that the compost is not tipping forward.

It is not at all necessary to stick to the conventional shapes for your baskets. Let your imagination wander and I am sure you will see the possibilities of making baskets of your own shape and design with all types of materials. Square wooden baskets made with slats of cedar wood, for example, look particularly attractive.

If you do not wish to confine your baskets to fuchsias there are many other plants which will be complemented by and complementary to them. The blue of the lobelia and the white of the allysum, together with begonias (both *pendulus* and *semperflorum*), pelargoniums, *impatiens* ('Busy Lizzy'), and various foliage plants are all useful in this respect.

Other Containers

Troughs of fuchsias and other plants free-standing on the patio can be very effective, and it is possible to use plants trained in upright forms, standards, pyramids, and so on, to give added height. Specimen plants such as these, with other plants being used as compost coverers, are very useful. A great deal of imagination can be used to find the right type of containers, and any ideas you have to produce some novel container will not be wasted. For example, a wooden wheelbarrow overflowing with flowers, or an old farm cart wheel used to support small half baskets, can be very effective.

So, you can use fuchsias wherever you want, or wherever you need to. If there is a hole in the patio paving put in a fuchsia, if you have a manhole to hide, cover it with a tub of fuchsias, and have fuchsias from the ground level right the way up to the eaves.

Recommended Cultivars for the Patio

The following is a short list of cultivars recommended for growing in pots and tubs on the patio. They will need to be taken inside during the winter for protection. This is a personal choice and it should be realised that any fuchsias can be used in this way – the variety is endless.

Annabel, Ann H. Tripp, Autumnale, Ballet Girl, Billy Green, Bon Accorde, Border Queen, Cambridge Louie, Celia Smedley, Cloverdale Pearl, Dark Eyes, Dollar Princess, Estelle Marie, Foxtrot, Joan Smith, Joy Patmore, King's Ransom, Marilyn Olsen, Margaret Pilkington, Mipam, Mrs Lovell Swisher, Pacquesa, Perry Park, Royal Velvet, Taddle, and Thalia.

The following is a short list of cultivars which have a lax type of growth and are therefore suitable for use in hanging baskets or wall baskets.

Annabel, Auntie Jinks, Cascade, Golden Marinka, Harry Gray, La Campanella, Marinka, Pink Galore, Pink Marshmallow, President Margaret Slater, President Stanley J. Wilson, and Swingtime.

GROWING PLANTS INDOORS

Many people are introduced to the pleasure of growing fuchsias as a result of having been given a plant in full flower, or there might even have been the temptation to purchase a flowering plant from a shop or at a flower show. Unfortunately, disappointment often follows when these plants arrive home, as the flowers start to fade and the new buds which had given so much hope for the future fall from the plant. You need to realise that fuchsias are not really house plants – they do not appreciate the dry conditions which we favour in our homes. In their natural environment on the wooded foothills of the mountains in South America, they have a constant humidity surrounding them. If you can emulate these conditions, which is what you are trying to do in the greenhouse where higher humidity is welcome, your plants will thrive. So, should fuchsias be taken into the home, and is it possible to grow them under those conditions?

The answer can be 'yes' on both counts. However, having a fuchsia indoors will be a temporary pleasure, as it is much better to bring in a full flowering plant, enjoy its beauty for a short period, and then return it to recuperate in a more appropriate environment. To make its temporary visit less traumatic you can try to give it a certain amount of humidity through its branches, and in this respect you cannot do much better than to follow the example of the growers of African Violets (*Saintpaulia*). An earthenware saucer or tray, somewhat larger than the base of the flower pot containing your plant, should be filled with gravel or pebbles. Water is added, so that the pot is standing upon moist pebbles, without the base actually being in contact with water. Standing the flower pot in a saucer of water will cause considerable damage and perhaps death to the root system, but the evaporation of the water from the pebble-filled saucer will give the necessary humidity through the branches of the plant, and it will be much happier for it. The same result could be achieved by spraying the leaves of the plant on a daily basis (although this can be damaging to the surrounding furniture if great care is not taken).

The loss of leaves and new flower buds from your plant bought in full flower is caused by a drastic change of environment, with the plant being taken from the perfect growing conditions of a greenhouse into the dry atmosphere of the home. If a plant has been grown within the drier

Fig 48   Plants growing indoors on a tray containing gravel.

atmosphere of the home from a very early stage, there is no reason why it should not develop fully and flower to perfection. Many people have success in maintaining small collections of fuchsias under these conditions.

For success indoors, it will be necessary to start at a very early stage in the development of the plant, the cutting stage. It is possible to root cuttings on the window-sill and these, with careful attention to their watering, potting, feeding and turning, can develop into good-sized plants. The window-sill of a bathroom would be an ideal situation, with the frosting of the glass cutting out the strong hot glare of the sun, and the atmosphere remaining moist.

Careful attention needs to be paid to the amount of light available to the plants. Each plant should be turned a quarter turn each day, so that all sides receive the same amount of light, and elongation of the branches on one side only will not occur. The natural desire of plants is always to grow towards the light.

Regular inspection for watering will be needed and, as all plants will undoubtedly be standing in a plant saucer, it might be advisable to water by pouring into the saucer. If you pour water into the top of the pot it is easy to be over-generous, and make the saucer overflow when the water has drained through the compost. Plants should be allowed to stand in the water in

Fig 49   A variety of fuchsias by a pond, including 'Vera Wolyn', 'Thalia', 'Harry Gray' and 'Caroline'.'

Fig 50   'Liebriez', a semi-double fuchsia.

58

the saucer for approximately fifteen minutes, giving them time to soak up all they need, and surplus water should then be poured away. If the compost in the pot has been allowed to dry out completely, difficulty will be experienced in encouraging the compost to 'take up' the water in the saucer – remember, a damp cloth will soak up much more water than a dry cloth. To overcome this difficulty it is advisable to immerse the pot completely in a bucket or bowl of water until all air bubbles cease to rise. It is to be hoped that by regular attention to the watering such a situation will not arise.

On a regular basis, perhaps once a week, the plants should be either placed in the bath or taken outside and given a thorough spraying over the foliage. This will help to free the pores of the leaves from dust and will add to the humidity around the plant. At the same time the tips of each plant should be carefully examined for any pests. Indoors greenfly seems to appear from nowhere and regular treatment will keep this sap-sucking insect at bay. White fly can also be a problem which can only be resolved by regular attention. Any good insecticide spray can be used for this purpose, and there are some special formulations for indoor plants. Read the label carefully to ensure that it is not unsafe to use inside or on fuchsias.

As the roots of the plants fill their pots they should be re-potted into the next size of pot. Always aim to move your plants into a pot no more than 1in (2.5cm) larger than the previous one. Your favourite peat-based compost will be ideal for this purpose, to give your plants fresh material into which the roots can work. When the pot becomes full of roots and nutrients become scarce, the plant will feel threatened and flower buds will be formed so that seeds can be set to continue the life of the species. While the potting-on process is taking place there will be no need to be feeding your plants as the new compost will provide all the extra nutrients required. However, when your plants have reached their final size of pot (in the first season of any plant a 5in (13cm) pot is sufficient), a feeding programme needs to be started.

The feeding will follow the same pattern as that recommended for greenhouse plants – a high nitrogen feed in the spring and early summer, a good balanced feed during the summer months, and a high potash feed later in the summer when the plants start to show their flowering buds. The recommended strength of feeding is always shown on the packet or bottle, and should never be exceeded. However, a greater dilution of feed used at each watering will have beneficial effects – try a quarter strength feeding at each watering.

Any fuchsia should be suitable for growing under these conditions but it might be advisable to concentrate upon those which have short compact growth and smaller flowers. The larger, more flamboyant flowers tend to be rather straggly in their growth and would become unmanageable within the confines of the home. When visiting shows or displays of fuchsias it might be as well to make a note of those cultivars which have the dwarfer growing habit and obtain these.

Recommended Cultivars for Indoor Growing

Bambini, Chang, Dusky Beauty, Frank Saunders, Lady Patricia Mountbatten, Marilyn Olsen, Mini-rose, Nellie Nuttall, Other Fellow, Saturnus, String of Pearls, Tom West, and Waveney Gem.

CHAPTER 6

The Seasons

WINTER CARE

Probably the question most frequently asked of experts is 'How do I look after my plants during the winter?' In answer to this, the important thing to remember is that fuchsias, being tender plants, will not tolerate frost. After the first severe frost the plants will be completely defoliated, and there may well be damage to the main structure of branches. With a prolonged cold spell all top growth is likely to be completely killed. However, if the root system is well protected from the frost, either by being some distance beneath the surface of the soil or within a building, it is unlikely to be affected and when warmth and moisture increase in the spring, it will produce fresh young shoots to replace those lost.

Plants which have been established in the garden will hopefully have been planted so that

Fig 51   'President Leo Boullemier' in a pot by a pond.

Fig 52   'Loeky'.

the rootball is several inches beneath the surface of the soil. When planting a new bed of hardy fuchsias it is always recommended that the surface of the rootball in the pot should be approximately 2in (5cm) beneath the level of the soil, to give some considerable insulation from any severe frosts that may occur. During the course of the summer it is possible that some of the surface soil will be washed away from around the base of the plants. In late autumn this can be replaced with fresh soil or with peat, and if you have a coal fire you could put well-washed ashes around the base of each plant. The main aim is to add extra insulation. Following the first severe frost, when the plants become defoliated, there will be the temptation to remove all the dead-looking branches in order to tidy up

the garden. You should not do this. Leave these branches in place, as they will serve two purposes. Firstly, they will remind you of the position of the fuchsia plants and thus discourage the possibility of disturbance by digging or planting bulbs; and secondly, these branches will afford some additional protection to the root system from heavy frosts. In the spring, when fresh growth starts, you can hope to see fresh young shoots growing around the base of these old branches. When this happens you will be able to remove those old stems and your garden will once again be in pristine condition.

The question is often asked whether there are certain varieties of fuchsia which can be left out during the winter. It is true that some have proved their hardiness over the years, for example, many which have the *Magellanica* species in their family tree. However, most people would be surprised at the large number of apparently tender cultivars, with lovely pastel shade flowers, which have survived even fairly severe winters in the open garden. Perhaps all plants should be given the opportunity to show just how hardy they are – give them as much protection as you can, and you may be pleasantly surprised. It is impossible to give a list of 'hardy fuchsias' as there are so many different factors. What is tender for one garden will be hardy in another, or even in another part of the same garden. So, give them all a try, record your successes, and note particularly the date upon which each of your plants shows its first flower. I suppose a good definition of a hardy fuchsia would be one which in the winter loses its leaves, but which in the warmer weather of spring sends up fresh young shoots from the root system, sufficiently early and strongly for flowers to be available during July.

Plants growing in tubs on the patio also need attention in the winter. It will be appreciated that as the root system is contained within a pot or tub it is highly likely that, without protection, the whole of the soil in that tub will become a solid frozen mass following a severe frost. The root system of any plant is unlikely to survive such conditions, and you should therefore make efforts to place such containers in a frost-free place where they are not likely to be affected. A garage or shed which can be kept frost-free, the spare room, an attic if it is well insulated, beneath the staging of a greenhouse if the temperature is maintained at or above the freezing point level, all these are places where your plants can survive. In the garden you make sure that the root system is beneath the surface of the soil, and let the soil be your insulation, and you can do the same for plants in pots by burying them in a trench in the garden. The deeper they are the more protection they will get. If you do 'inter' your plants in this way make sure that you cover the old branches with straw or peat, and that you mark the position of the pot (for obvious

Fig 53 *Defoliated plant being prepared for winter storage with gentle pruning.*

reasons). Before carrying out this operation the plants should be completely defoliated, and slightly trimmed back by about one-third of the total length, so that they are more easily manageable. When this defoliation and trimming have been completed, give the whole plant a spray with a combined insecticide and fungicide spray.

Those plants which are accessible during the winter will need attention and watering. Plants which are being kept in their containers in, for example, a spare room should also have been defoliated and trimmed back. They too need a good spraying with insecticide and fungicide, but in addition the rootball should be kept in a 'just moist' condition. Under no circumstances should the rootball be allowed to dry out completely. More plants have been lost during the winter because their root systems have died through lack of moisture than because they were kept

Fig 54   Storing plants over the winter in a 'grave' in the garden.

too moist. You need to examine your plants regularly during the winter, perhaps once a week, to ensure that the compost is kept just moist. Try not to allow the temperature in which they have been stored to rise too greatly – you don't want your plants to grow, you want them to remain in a semi-dormant state. If you have stacked your plants in large boxes and have protected them with sheets of newspaper, it may be difficult to examine them regularly, but an effort should be made at least a couple of times during the winter months.

When you are in the position to be able to give your plants additional warmth and light, they can be removed from their winter quarters and encouraged to start back into growth. However, do not be tempted to do this at too early a stage if you are unable to maintain the steady tem-

perature that is necessary. March might be early enough to remove the plants that you interred in the garden, and you might well be surprised to see masses of thin straggly white shoots growing from the branches. This simply means your plants are alive. You will need to prune the top growths back fairly hard to encourage new growth from lower down, but at least you will know that your plants have come through the winter successfully.

All container-grown plants, pots, tubs or hanging baskets, need this type of protection, unless you are able to maintain within a greenhouse a temperature of a minimum of 40°F (5°C). At this temperature the plants will not grow but will just 'tick over' in a semi-dormant state. Leaves will remain on the branches, although many will turn yellow and will fall. These

Fig 55 'Ting-a-ling'.

should be removed so that the risk of botrytis (grey mould) will be reduced. The soil of these plants should be kept just moist. When the temperatures rise and the light intensity improves, such plants will be the first to show signs of new vigour.

Great care should also be taken of plants which have been trained into other shapes, such as standards, fans and pyramids. Under no circumstances should these be left out in the garden – the first severe frost will kill all the top growth that you have so carefully trained over a long period of time. With a standard the important part is the stem. If that is killed, you will have fresh growth (with luck) growing from the base,

but you will have lost your standard shape. If you have standards growing in the garden during the summer (and there is no better way to get additional height to your bedding schemes), these plants will have to be lifted in the autumn, before risk of frosts, and be given protection inside. The same sort of treatment will therefore be given to these as you give to your container-grown plants. A difficulty arises from the awkwardness of their shape, and the amount of space they will take, but you can reduce this by judicious pruning. Tidy up the rootball as much as possible, cutting back any long, straggly and perhaps damaged roots – a dusting with a fungicide powder might be beneficial at this stage. The whole rootball can then be wrapped in hessian or some other substance to prevent soil from being scattered. The top growth of standards can also be reduced in size, perhaps by as much as a half, so that they can more easily be stored.

For storing, standards can be laid down under the staging of a greenhouse and covered with newspaper to give protection from severe frosts if the greenhouse is not heated. Newspaper, or polystyrene tiles beneath the plants, will give additional protection. Again it will be necessary to examine the rootballs during the course of the winter to prevent them from becoming too dry. Moistness is your objective once again. Large structures such as fans, pyra-

mids, pillars, and so on, all present their additional problems, and each grower of these specialist shapes will need to devise some method of ensuring a frost-free environment through the winter.

SPRING

One of the greatest pleasures of being involved with plants is derived from always looking forward, and the anticipation of things to come helps you through the dark, damp days of the early year. In the fuchsia calendar you can start your 'New Year' whenever you wish, according to the facilities available to you, and this will

Fig 56   'Harry Gray'.

involve revitalising your old plants which have been over-wintering in a semi-dormant state.

If you have the facilities to maintain a temperature in excess of 45°F (7°C), the earlier you can start the better. Remove your plants from their winter quarters and examine them carefully. If you have been examining them through the winter, and have ensured that the compost is just moist and the rootballs frost-free, you can assume that the plants will still be alive. To make sure, there are two tasks which need to be done now and which will indicate the success or otherwise of your over-wintering activities. First, you will need to prune back the branches even further than you did for storing. Using a sharp pair of secateurs, cut back each branch so that there are just two sets of leaf nodes on each branch – the centre of each branch should look

green and sappy. If the centre of the branch is brown and brittle, that branch is dead. A simple test that you can carry out before you start to prune your plant is to scratch the surface of the branch with your thumb nail. If, when you have removed the top layer of skin, you see greenness and sappiness, then success has been achieved.

The second task is to remove the plant from its pot and to replace all the old compost with fresh. All the old compost should be teased away from the root system – the pointed end of a flower stick is ideal for this purpose. (Try not to damage any young white roots that may be showing – these are further proof of successful over-wintering.) You might find it easier to remove the old compost by swilling the whole root system in a bucket of water. Once the old

Fig 57   (a) Pruning for new growth. (b) Root pruning prior to re-potting.

compost has been removed it is possible to examine the root system. Remove with secateurs any old gnarled roots which have served their purpose and have coiled around the pot. You can be fairly ruthless with this activity, but do try to maintain an even shape consisting of the young white roots.

The plant is now ready to be re-potted. Having been pruned the rootball will take up less space than previously, and it will therefore be possible to re-pot in a smaller pot. The experts call this 'potting back'. It should be possible to pot a plant from a 5 or 6in (12.5–15cm) pot into a 3½in (9cm) one. Use a pot of the correct size to hold the roots comfortably, and a compost which is fresh and of the type you normally favour. Place a small quantity in the bottom of the pot, hold the plant in position centrally with one hand, and trickle fresh compost around the

Fig 58   Spray the top branches daily to encourage the formation of new shoots.

roots with the other hand. A slight tapping of the pot on the bench every now and again will encourage the compost to permeate between the roots. Continue this process until the pot is full to the rim. Do not firm the compost with your fingers, but be content to settle the plant in the pot by tapping it on the bench. The compost should be just moist when being used, and the final settling can be carried out by watering the plants with the fine rose on a watering can. This watering should suffice for two or three weeks.

The plant will have suffered a traumatic experience in the branch and root pruning, and will therefore need a certain amount of pampering for a short while to assist in the formation of new roots. Place the newly-potted plant in the warmest spot in your greenhouse, or on a window-sill, shading initially from any hot sun. Daily attention will need to be paid to spraying the young pruned branches with pure, tepid water, and if you can do this two or three times a day the plants will benefit. This will be the only watering that the plant will require, the excess from the branches falling on to the compost to keep it in a just moist condition. This overhead spraying will soften the top surface of the branches and will encourage the young dormant shoots in the leaf axils to grow.

Two or three weeks should be sufficient to see a complete change in your plant. The new pink buds will appear and it will be obvious, because of the growth up above, that there is growth of the roots down below. When all the branches are showing new growth, it is possible to carry out a final, delicate pruning session, cutting branches back to a strong growing shoot, and thus shaping the plant to your requirements.

It should be possible to remove any shading after growth is visible, and to start normal watering. The new compost will contain nutrients so it should not be necessary to feed your plants for the first three or four weeks. Thereafter you should use a liquid fertiliser, diluted to about a quarter of the normal recommended strength.

With rapid new top growth you can be

Fig 59   'Margaret Roe'.

assured of the rapid growth of roots. It will therefore be necessary to examine the compost in the pot quite regularly, by inverting the pot and holding the complete rootball on your hand, to ensure that the roots have not completely filled the pot. You should see the fresh young white roots at the edge of the compost, but you do not want them to start circling the base of the pot. When the roots are easily visible consideration should be given to moving the plant into a larger pot.

There is always discussion amongst growers as to whether the root pruning and the top pruning should be carried out at the same time. Many recommend re-potting and root pruning the plant in one operation, and then carrying out

the task of top or branch pruning when the new growths are visible. Many feel that the double shock in one operation is too traumatic for the plant. I personally favour carrying out both operations at the same time and have never lost any plants as a result of doing so. However, there are no set rules in the growing of fuchsias that you absolutely have to follow.

Plants interred in the garden should be left in that position (unless you have warm facilities into which you can place them) until the beginning of March. When you remove them from their 'grave', there may be long straggly white growths in evidence. These are of no use and should be removed. In fact, once they have been dug out, these plants can be treated in the same way as

68

Fig 60 'Winston Churchill'.

Fig 61   Fuchsia fulgens.

the others. Heavy pruning of the top growth will ensure that all those straggly white shoots are removed.

Standards, or other trained shapes, which have been in a semi-dormant 'green leaf' state during the winter (kept just alive but not really growing), can be also treated in the same way. The top growths will need to be pruned drastically, back to two or three nodes on each branch. You need to encourage as much fresh growth as possible from a tight head on the standard, so pruning back hard is essential. As you will be encouraging all this fresh growth in the head, you must also encourage growth of the roots down below. The process should be carried out to remove the old compost and to replace it with fresh, the roots should be pruned, and the plant re-potted in either a new pot of the same size or a pot one size smaller. Again, overhead spraying to encourage fresh young shoots should be carried out on a daily basis.

Standards which were allowed to become denuded of leaves, or were over-wintered buried or lying under the staging of a greenhouse, will need additional treatment to encourage those dormant buds in the leaf axils to grow.

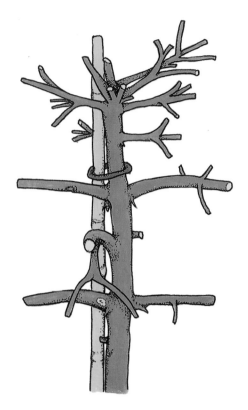

Fig 63   'Checkerboard'.

Fig 62   Hard pruning of the top growth of a standard head in order to encourage fresh shoots.

They should be pruned as recommended and sprayed as often as possible. If the new growth is uneven – this often happens – the buds can be encouraged to 'break' by lying the standard on the bench with the undeveloping buds upper-most. Regular spraying should then encourage those buds to start into growth. Once the standards start to grow it is important to encourage even growth by regularly turning the plant so that all sides get an equal share of the light. This also applies to the bush or shrub trained plants. One method of ensuring that all sides of the plant benefit is to have the labels of all the plants facing in the same direction, training yourself always to turn the plants in a clockwise direction, and always seeing that the labels are facing in the same direction on each plant. A quarter turn

each day will be sufficient to encourage even growth.

Plants growing in baskets can either be treated as individual plants, removed from the basket and grown on separately, or treated as a whole. For the latter it will be necessary to remove the complete rootball from the basket, tease away as much of the old compost as possible (or remove the bottom couple of inches by cutting with a carving knife), and replace with fresh compost. Overhead spraying will encourage the fresh growths.

Do not be frightened about cutting back hard into the old wood. If you remember that fuchsias will only form flowers on wood that has been grown in the current season, you will be encour-aged·to get as much fresh wood as possible, leaving only the minimum of old wood to help form the foundation for the new. You have to be cruel to be kind.

71

CHAPTER 7

Pests and Diseases

Fuchsia growers are very lucky in that they are not troubled with a great many pests and diseases. The few that there are are quite easily controlled, but of course it is far better not to allow such conditions to get hold. Prevention is always better than cure. One of the most important suggestions always made to beginners growing fuchias is not to grow too many plants. This advice is valid in that, if fewer plants are grown, it becomes possible to handle each of them regularly and so any pests or diseases are detected at a very early stage.

PESTS

Greenfly

Greenfly can usually be seen in clusters around the light green tip of each shoot. They are unmistakable in appearance and cause damage to plants in that they are sap-sucking insects, and

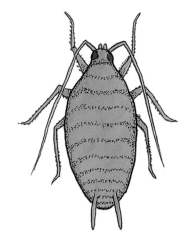

Fig 65 An aphid.

Fig 64 Aphids.

Fig 66 Greenfly.

this action causes distortion and curling of the young leaves. They are very prolific in their reproductive habits so quick action is advisable. Regular spraying with an insecticide such as 'Tumblebug' or 'Spray Day' will keep the green-fly at bay, but I must stress the word regular. There are many old-fashioned remedies for dealing with this pest – if you know of one, and it seems to work well for you, then continue to use it.

White Fly

White fly are extremely troublesome and un-fortunately the fuchsia seems to be a particular favourite of this pest. These white flies are easily seen by looking under the upper leaves of plants. Again, they can be controlled by spraying, but unfortunately the sprays are only effective against the adult flies. The eggs are not affected, so it is necessary to keep spraying at intervals of about four days in order to destroy the newly-emerging adults before they can lay further eggs. If a four-day spraying programme is carried out even a severe infection can be eradicated in a couple of weeks. The earlier a possible invasion by white flies is discovered, the easier it will be to stamp it out, so regular inspections are the order of the day. When there are only a couple of flies a finger and thumb technique is very satisfactory and satisfying.

Red Spider

Red spider mites are, I suppose, one of the worst type of pests for fuchsias. They are very difficult to detect in the early stages and are, in fact, almost invisible to the naked eye through-out their life span. Plants which have been attacked by the red spider mite (not a spider at all really) can be easily recognised, as the foliage turns to a bronze colour and becomes very brittle. In later stages very fine webs can be seen spreading from leaf to leaf. This pest is very contagious and rapidly spreads to many plants in a greenhouse. It is often considered that an

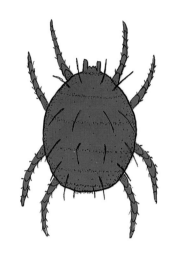

Fig 67   Red spider mite.

attack of red spider mite results from poor growing conditions. The mite thrives in a hot, dry atmosphere so if your plants are growing in the correct type of conditions for fuchsias (warm and moist), you are unlikely to suffer severely from it. Plants which are affected should be removed from close proximity to others and thoroughly sprayed with a good systemic insecti-cide. All plants in the greenhouse should be sprayed regularly.

Fig 68   Red spider mite web.

73

Fig 69   Capsid bugs.

Capsid Bug

On plants which are growing outside you may come across another pest which causes disfiguration of the growing tips – the capsid bug. This is another sap-sucking insect which punctures the young leaves, causing them to blister and turn red. Spraying with insecticide will again rectify the position. It is easy to forget the possibility of plants which are bedded out in the garden being attacked, but I am afraid this very often happens, especially if the plants are bedded under, or in close proximity to, larger trees.

Sciarid Flies

Unfortunately with the advent of the soilless (peat-based) composts we seem to have imported these small black flies, which lay their eggs in it. The damage is done by the emerging larvae which will eat the roots of cuttings or seedlings. They rarely affect mature plants, although their presence can be rather annoying.

Watering the affected compost with a solution of malathion or stirring some gamma-HCH powder into the top of the compost will have the effect of destroying this pest. Over-watering of peat-based composts encourages the presence of these pests.

Vine Weevil

The vine weevil larva is one pest which seems to have become far more prevalent in recent years, and that prevalence seems to coincide with the advent of peat-based composts. The adult is a black, beetle-like insect and is nocturnal in its habits. The first sign of the presence of the adult vine weevil is when notches are seen to have been eaten from the edge of leaves – at first you might feel tempted to blame caterpillars. The greatest damage though is done, not by the adult beetle but by the larvae. The eggs are laid in the surface of the compost and when hatched they produce a grub which is about ½in (1cm) in length, whitish with a brownish head.

Fig 70   Larva of the vine weevil.

These grubs burrow down into the compost and feed off the young white roots, doing untold damage to the young plants. Many cures are suggested for vine weevils but malathion soaked into the compost seems to be very effective. Potting back the older plants in the early spring is a good time to discover whether any grubs are present. Again, prevention is better than cure – the adults being nocturnal need hiding places by day and rubbish under the staging of greenhouses is very much to their liking.

DISEASES

Botrytis Cineria

Botrytis is one of the two main diseases of which you need to be aware. It is very easily identified by the grey, rather hairy-like mould. This can be caused by dank, airless conditions, the rotting of dying foliage, and a general lack of air circulation. The temptation to grow too many plants too closely packed together promotes the conditions for the growth of this disease. The cure is good circulation of air (vents open throughout the year if possible), and the prevention of cold, damp, stagnant conditions. If plants are affected by botrytis then they should be sprayed with a

Fig 71   Botrytis.

good systemic fungicide or, if the weather is cold and this would only add to the damp conditions, dusted with a fungicide powder.

Rust

Fuchsia rust is another disease which has become far more noticeable in recent years. It is very debilitating and is very easily transmitted from one plant to another. It is readily identified by reddish-brown markings (rings) on the upper side of leaves, while on the underside typical orangey-brown pustules can be seen – in fact, it looks exactly like rust. Unfortunately the spores on the underside of the leaves can be passed from one plant to another purely by the movement of air currents, and also on the hands of the grower or by insects.

The cure for an attack of rust is firstly to remove any infected plants from the presence of other plants. Try to remove any of the leaves which have the tell-tale marks and *burn* them. The whole plant should then be sprayed with a good fungicide such as 'Nimrod T', or 'Plantvax 75' if you can get hold of it. Keep the treated plants separate from others and keep a very careful eye on all plants, removing any affected leaves as soon as the first signs show.

Unfortunately, plants bearing rust spores are sometimes first brought into the greenhouse from the collections of others. It is a wise precaution to place any newly-acquired plants in quarantine for a couple of weeks and thus make sure they are not affected. At one stage experts would have advised the complete burning of any affected plant, but modern methods are not quite so drastic.

The general advice, then, is to spray your affected plants with a suitable insecticide or fungicide. But this is not the only method of removing the offending pests or diseases. In fact, it would be unwise to use wet sprays on your plants when they are in full flower, as the sprays would cause marking and damage to the flowers and buds. I would always recommend using wet sprays at the beginning of the season before buds are well formed, and at the end of the season when plants have been prepared for their winter rests. Always read the instructions very carefully before mixing your sprays. Follow the instructions and do not think that if you use a spray stronger than that recommended you will get better results. You will only be wasting money, and you could easily damage the foliage of the plants. As most of the sprays only affect the adult pests it will be necessary to undertake a programme of spraying at intervals of three or four days until the infestation has been cleared. Most pests hide themselves under the leaves of the plants so you must ensure that *all* parts of the plants are well moistened. If the spray you are using is of a systemic variety it will give prolonged protection from the pests or diseases, as the chemical is absorbed through the leaves of the plant and remains in the sap. I would always recommend using a systemic type insecticide or fungicide if one is available.

It is also possible now to obtain insecticide 'pins'. These are pushed into the soil at the base of the plant and the chemical is absorbed by the plant through the root system. This is especially useful when the plants are in flower or if you have just a few special plants for show purposes. It is not the cheapest method of fending off pests, but a simple and very effective one when just a few plants are involved.

It is also possible to purchase 'smoke bombs' or 'cones', which contain a fungicide or insecticide, released as a cloud of smoke when they are ignited. These again are very effective at the time of the year when flowers or buds are present, but it does mean closing off the greenhouse and making it as airtight as possible to stop the smoke escaping before the cure has been effected. At the time of the year when we will most need this, the days are likely to be hot and all the ventilation possible is usually being given to the plants. However, if it is possible to carry out the smoking last thing at night, it should be most effective. During damp, cold days in late autumn

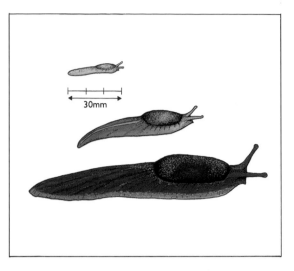

Fig 72 Fuchsias are also vulnerable to attack from slugs. These are the three common varieties; the garden slug (the smallest), the keeled slug and the black slug (the largest).

or early winter, when the atmosphere is heavily laden with moisture and we are anxious not to increase the level of dampness in the greenhouse by spraying, this method of curing the ills is most useful.

On the same principle, but advancing a stage further, it is possible to fix up fumigators or vapourisers in your greenhouse. These are rather more expensive but are extremely effective.

If you have only a few plants, and are growing them indoors on the window-sill, don't try to spray whilst they are still indoors. Badly infected plants should be taken outside and given a good spraying. Alternatively, if an infestation is only in its early stages, it is possible to hold the foliage in a bowl of soapy water. This will wash off any aphids which might be present. Insecticide sticks pressed into the compost around the edge of the pot will keep pests at bay.

One final word of warning – keep all chemicals safely locked away. They can be very dangerous to children and to animals. Never keep any 'mixed up' sprays in either bottles or the sprayer – when you have completed your spraying tasks, dispose of the remainder.

CHAPTER 8

Fuchsia Calendar

JANUARY

It is tempting at this time of year to sit back and think that everything is all right. Do not be lulled into a false sense of security – plants still need to be looked at. January is probably the severest of all months, especially to those plants which have been stored for the winter. See that all protective material is still in position, especially if no heat is being used in your place of storage. If the opportunity presents itself, remove the plants from their store and examine them carefully. Do not allow the compost in the pots (or round the roots, if stored in boxes) to become bone dry. A

little moisture added now will keep the roots alive, although growth up above is to be discouraged. Remove any debris that there may be around the plants.

Towards the end of the month, if you require early plants and are able to provide some heat, you will be able to start those plants into fresh life. It will be necessary, though, to provide a good steady heat, so don't start them into growth until absolutely necessary.

If you are providing heat throughout the winter, your summer- or autumn-struck cuttings will be continuing to grow steadily. Don't be tempted to give them too much heat or you will,

Fig 73   Spraying plants which have been in winter storage. Remember to replace their protective material.

Fig 74   *Watering and spraying autumn-rooted cuttings.*

as a result of the lack of light intensity, have plants which are rather straggly and drawn. These young plants need to be kept growing just steadily in a temperature of 45°F (7°C). Do not feed your young plants at this time of the year, even if they are looking a little pale and wan.

Examine the young plants carefully for any pests or diseases that might be present – remember that the conditions liked by your plants are also loved by pests, and they will multiply. Spraying at this time of the year is not recommended, so take care of the pests by using smoke cones or insecticide sticks. Don't encourage too moist an atmosphere. Remove any leaves which have died or are yellowing – a dead leaf falling across a branch could easily lead to the loss of the whole branch.

During this month it is possible to get bright sunny days. The weather may be cold, but the sun shining through the glass will raise the temperature inside the greenhouse quite considerably. As often as possible keep the door and vents open so that there is a healthy flow of air. Good air ventilation will help to prevent botrytis. If you do open all the windows, remember to close them again early in the afternoon so that the temperature does not fall too dramatically. An investment in automatic ventilators really repays itself at this time of the year.

On one of those bright sunny days examine the plants that are still out in the garden. If you protected the crown of the plants with peat, well-weathered ashes, bracken or some such other insulation in the autumn, ensure that it is still in position and renew it if necessary.

During the many inclement days which are often experienced during this month, take the opportunity of giving some thought to the situation regarding the materials you will be requiring during the coming season. In the comfort of your sitting room you can look through the gardening magazines and plan for the future. On a bright day you could ensure that the pots and trays you have in store are in a good clean condition and ready for use. Supplies of compost should be considered and ordered if necessary. Labels,

Fig 75   Garden plants over-wintering outdoors with protective material on the ground around the base.

canes, pots, ties, insecticides, fungicides, feeds and so on should be examined and lists made for ordering when possible.

Write off to suppliers of plants for their catalogues and send in your orders as soon as possible to stand a good chance of getting what you want.

January can be a dismal month, but you can see it as full of promise for the future.

FEBRUARY

Beware this month. Promises of things to come one day can be removed with a vengeance the following day. We can expect to have periods of good sunny days when the temperatures will soar, especially in the greenhouse, and then, with clear skies during the night, the temperature will plummet. Damp weather plus heavy falls of snow can be expected, so you must be prepared to maintain the correct temperature in the greenhouse.

Plants over-wintering in an unheated position should be examined carefully at the beginning of the month to ensure that they are still in good condition. Do not allow the compost to become

bone dry, but add a little moisture to that area when conditions permit. Towards the end of the month it might be necessary to provide some heat to start those plants into growth. Consider partitioning off a small part of a greenhouse which you will be able to heat to a higher temperature. If this is possible, take your resting plants out of storage, tidy them up slightly by cutting back some of the straggly wood, place them in a warm position and spray overhead. This spraying will encourage the young dormant shoots in the leaf axils to soften up and start to grow. Only slight additional watering to the rootball is necessary at this time. With the production of the young shoots in the axils you will be able to cut back the top growth and start the shaping of your plants. Protect these plants, especially the young shoots, from any severe drop in the temperature that might occur at night. Sheets of newspaper over the plants will help to trap the heat and will protect them. Remove the newspaper by day so that they receive the maximum amount of light possible.

Fig 76   Pruning the top growth and root pruning of stored plants. The plants can then be sprayed to encourage the formation of shoots.

Conversely though, on extremely bright sunny days, and it is not unknown in February, keep the plants shaded from the extreme brightness.

Ventilation is again of paramount importance. Ventilate as often as the opportunity arises, and keep a healthy flow of air passing through the greenhouse on bright days.

Young plants from summer and autumn cuttings will be growing apace now. Give them as much light as possible, and don't over-heat them. Try to handle and examine each plant regularly. Those plants which are being grown for bushes should have their growing tips removed as soon as they have reached the required length (usually two or three pairs of leaves). Plants growing as standards should be allowed to grow upright; make sure that a split cane is in position and that the growing whip is tied to it between each pair

Fig 77   'Aunty Jinks'.

of leaves. Remove any side shoots that form in the lower leaf axils at an early stage. Keep an eye open for pests and diseases, and spray if necessary on dry days – do this as early in the day as possible so that there is not an excess of moisture around when frosts return at night. Examine the rootballs of these young plants, and if they have filled their pots with roots, pot them on into the next size of pot. A feed of perhaps quarter strength might be appreciated, but do not over-feed. As you handle the plants examine the labels – any which are becoming faint should be replaced.

Get ready for the cutting season. Make sure that your propagator is in good working order, or that you have sufficient propagators for your purposes. Cuttings taken at the end of this month will provide excellent plants for show work in 3½in (9cm) or 5in (13cm) pots later in the season.

If you failed to do so last month, make sure your order is sent off to your specialist fuchsia nurseryman. Remember that it is better to see the young plants that you are buying rather than to depend upon a postal service, and if you have the chance you should collect your plants in person. Most nurseries are open for business at this time of the year and good young plants will be available which could form the basis of your show plants in the coming season.

If you can get out into the garden examine the crowns of any plants which are over-wintering there. If any of the protective material has been removed – wind and birds can do this – replace it. You will not see any growths coming up from the base just yet. Do not be tempted to cut back the old, dead top growth yet – leave that until there are signs of new life from below, as it does protect from the severest frosts. Replace the old labels if necessary.

MARCH

In March spring has almost arrived, and life is beginning to return to everything. To get the real

Fig 78 *'Aunty Jinks' grown as a bonsai.*

benefit from all those old plants which have been stored through the winter you must now get moving on them. Prune back some of the top growth, and give them regular overhead sprays with tepid water. Keep them in the warmest place you can find (in the light), and encourage the little pink buds to appear from the leaf axils. Protect them from severe overnight frosts but give them as much light as possible by day. When the young shoots appear, prune back hard so that you are down to one or two shoots on each branch. Re-pot when they are showing this sign of growth into a pot a size or two smaller than the one from which they have been taken. Remove all the old compost – wash it off if necessary – and re-pot using fresh compost, having trimmed back any old and gnarled roots there may be. Keep the plants warm and humid to help them recover from this shock. Keep an eye open when re-potting for the larvae of the vine weevil. Failure to spot them now might well

mean that the new young roots of your plants will become a feast for them.

If plants look dead when you take them out of stock, test the bark by gently scraping the surface. If there is green tissue under the bark the plant is still alive, but if it is brown the possibility is that the branch is dead. Test all of the branches before finally discarding the plant.

When they are available start taking cuttings, labelling them carefully. Don't take too many, unless you wish to pass them on to friends. Cuttings which were taken last month might need potting into their first individual pots.

Keep a check on your stocks of compost, pots and labels – nothing is more infuriating than to run out when in the middle of an operation. Keep a check also on the space you are using in the greenhouse. If it is too full now you will have insufficient space when the plants really start growing.

Watch out for the signs of pests and diseases

taking over, and try to get into the habit of carrying out a regular pattern of spraying. Action taken now will keep you free from trouble later. Spray regularly but vary the spray you use, alternating with different types of insecticide so that the 'nasties' don't become immune to any one type.

Keep all vents open all day, unless frost is still threatening. As much air as possible circulating will help to keep the plants free from moisture-loving diseases such as botrytis.

Towards the end of the month, with the sun rising higher in the sky each day, it will be necessary to consider shading the plants from direct sunlight. There are a number of substances that can be painted on the glass and they are very successful for this purpose. You can invest in a sophisticated blind system if you wish.

Keep an eye on those plants that you are training to various shapes. The standard whips need to be kept growing straight and true, and regular neat tying is a necessity. Keep rubbing out the shoots in the leaf axils until you are approaching the height you require. Do not remove the leaves from the trunk until you have built up a very good head on your plant. Bush and shrub trained plants should be turned regularly and the growing tips pinched out to encourage good bushy plants. Every two or three pairs of leaves will be sufficient. If you want plants for enjoyment as opposed to showing, then two stops will be sufficient for your purposes. Plants for baskets should be growing apace. Keep them in their 3½in (9cm) pots, pinching them out at three pairs of leaves on each branch. Make sure that your baskets are ready for planting up – the sooner you can do this the sooner they will become established.

As often as possible – on good balmy March days – place your plants outside in the fresh air. They will enjoy it.

Examine the base of your outdoor plants. No shoots will be expected yet. Make sure that any protective material is still in position, and prepare the ground for planting out your new bed of hardies. Don't put them out yet, but leave them growing strongly in their pots under cover. The planting will be carried out in June.

APRIL

Spring is really with us in April, but do not be lulled into a false sense of security – it is still possible to have very cold nights and cold days. Remember that the north of Britain is two or three weeks 'behind' the south.

With the light intensifying each day, your plants will be growing apace, and the sun shining through the glass can cause quite a dramatic rise in the temperature within the greenhouse. Try to maintain a higher humidity within the greenhouse now by spraying water on the floor and between the pots. Care must be taken regarding the watering of your plants, as they will rapidly dry out if the temperature soars. If you have not put shading on the glass do so now, or fix blinds.

Make sure that your outside frame is ready to receive plants. Clear away any old pots and debris, freshen the surface of the soil, and give a thorough soaking with a disinfectant such as Jeyes Fluid – leave the frame light off and do not attempt to place any plants inside until the fumes have cleared. The frame will be used at the end of the month for hardening off plants which are destined for the open border.

Keep a very careful eye on the way your plants are growing. Try to handle each pot every day, as this will tell you if the plant requires watering. Treat each plant as an individual. Regularly turn each plant so that no one side has more of the sun than any other. Keep pinching out the growing tips as and when two or three pairs of leaves have formed. Standard whips should be reaching the height you require fairly soon – stop removing the side shoots as they approach the height, as these shoots will be required for the head of the plant.

Continue a regular spraying pattern for pests

Fig 79 (Opposite) A fuchsia half standard – 'Countess of Aberdeen'.

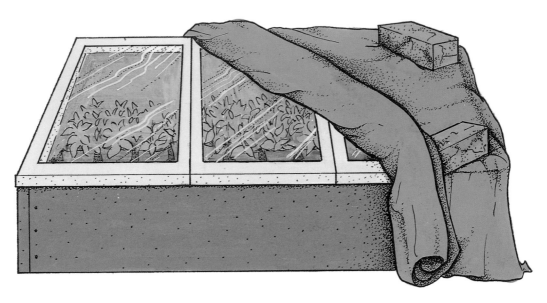

Fig 80   Garden frame with plants intended for bedding out growing inside,
protected from frost by a covering.

and diseases. Feeding will need to take priority –
regular feeding on a little and often basis will give
good strong healthy plants that are evenly
grown. At this time of the year you are building
up top growth and roots, so a feed containing a
higher proportion of nitrogen is the ideal.

Plants growing strongly in 3½in (9cm) or 5in
(13cm) pots needed for bedding display can be
hardened off in the cold frame towards the end
of April. Give them as much air as possible, but
leave the lights in position at the start. After a
week or two the lights can be removed during
warm days, especially if there are warm April
showers. At night make sure that the lights are in
position and, if a frost is threatened, give the
added protection of sheets of newspaper over
the plants inside the frame. Some growers line
their frames with polystyrene ceiling tiles early in
the season as insulation. If very severe frosts are
forecast, heavier insulation on the frame might
be necessary. If they are suffering from the cold,
some plants take on a distinctly blue hue on the
leaves.

If you are without a greenhouse and have
been storing your plants in boxes, in the garage,
or even buried in the ground, the beginning of
this month is the ideal time for you to examine
them and start to bring them back to life. Clean
them off completely and take them into the
warmth of the house and the light of a window.
Try to encourage the side shoots to form by
regular spraying (mind the furniture), and keep
turning them (several times a day if necessary).
Once the shoots have started to show, remove
each plant from its pot and re-pot into fresh
compost. Keep an eye open for any aphids that
might have over-wintered with your plants.
Once good strong fresh growth has been
started, get the plants into the fresh air as often
as you can.

Make sure that your hardy border is prepared for your plants. Dig deeply, incorporating
some good manure, and work in a handful or so
of bonemeal to each square yard. Remember
that once your plants are in position they will
remain *in situ* for a number of years. Don't stint
on this preparation or you may regret it.

Make up your baskets, but keep them in the
greenhouse, standing them on large pots on the
staging and only taking them outside when the

weather is very amenable. Keep pinching out the growing tips when three pairs of leaves have been formed. (Remember when you start removing growing tips you must remove all of those that can be seen.)

Any flowers which form now should be removed – they are not really true to form and will only serve to weaken the plants.

MAY

Everything is now growing rapidly and it is a job keeping up with all the tasks that present themselves. Some flowers are beginning to appear on the earliest of the plants. Keep a record of the plants which do this so that in the future the right type of plants can be grown for an early display.

All the over-wintered plants should be growing well now, and the potting back process should have been completed. If you were troubled with vine weevil, make a resolution to keep the area under the staging as clear as possible so that the beetles have nowhere to hide during the day. Keep a very careful eye open for any pests and diseases. Continue to spray regularly with both an insecticide and a fungicide.

Examine recently-purchased plants carefully. It is better to segregate them from your main collection until you are sure that they are clear of diseases. Be on the lookout particularly for signs of rust on your plants. This appears as small brown marks on the upper surface of leaves, and tell-tale orange-coloured pustules underneath. Remove any infected plants, dispose of the affected leaves and spray thoroughly with a good fungicide. Dip the whole plant, including the pot, in a solution of this fungicide. Watch carefully for any signs of a return of the rust on that plant, and on others which were in its vicinity.

The days are getting longer, the sun is higher, and the temperature is more consistent. Do not be tempted to remove all the heat from your houses, especially at night. The beginning of the

Fig 81   Shade the greenhouse to keep the temperature down on hot days, and leave open the door and vents to ensure air circulation.

Fig 82   Ruthless pruning of hardy plants growing in a permanent site in the garden.

mulch of well-rotted farmyard manure, or a sprinkling of bonemeal around the base of each plant, will help the plant to build up a good structure for the coming season. Remember that through the season it will be beneficial to give these plants a regular feeding of your usual liquid fertiliser.

Plants hardening off in the cold frame for planting out should be moved into 5in (13cm) pots if they have filled their present pots with roots. Do not, even in the south, be tempted to plant out your hardies until the very end of May or the beginning of June. Plant them deeply when you do, a couple of inches below the level of the compost in the pot.

Keep up a regular pattern of feeding both your pot plants and your border plants. A feeding at dilute strength every time you water will be beneficial. Do not feed a plant that is ailing. Discover the cause of the discontent and correct this before feeding. A plant that has been suffering at the roots for any reason could benefit from foliar feeding.

Continue to pinch out the growing tips of the plants if you want bushy plants for a specific date, but bear in mind that you need to leave eight

month can be treacherous. If the night temperature is forecast at 39°F (4°C) or less, keep the heat on. By day keep all vents and doors open so that air can circulate freely, and on hot days try to maintain a humid atmosphere and keep the temperature down by spraying the pathways and the benches. Examine the shading that you painted on the glass – it will probably require an extra coating now.

In the border, remove any of the winter protection that is still in position. Examine the base of the plants carefully – with luck new growths will be starting to show. If the winter has been mild and shoots are appearing on the upper parts of the branches, do not be tempted to leave them, as you will only have rather unsightly bare stems lower down on your plants. Encourage growth from as low down as possible by cutting back the old wood now, so that only a couple of shoots are left on each branch. A good

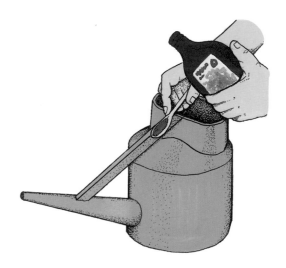

Fig 83   Never exceed the manufacturer's recommendations when measuring out feeds.

weeks for single-flowered varieties and ten weeks for double-flowered plants before they will come into flower. At the beginning of this month it might not be a bad idea to look at the show dates, and work backwards from there to ascertain the last possible date upon which you should pinch out your plants. The times given are only a general guide – depending upon prevailing weather conditions you may need longer.

Continue to train the heads of your standards, and try to get them as evenly-shaped as you possibly can. Consider the size of pot that they are in. Usually standards of the larger types, the half standards and the full standards, can be shown in any size of pot. If they become pot-bound at any stage of their growth, the standards will want to flower. The possibility of shaping the head diminishes as soon as flower buds start to appear.

Think ahead to next year. If the conditions that you are able to offer your plants during the winter are conducive to continuous steady growth, you might consider growing some plants on the biennial method. Briefly, this is growing the plants one year and flowering them the next. You will require a minimum temperature of 40–45°F (7–8°C) to be maintained throughout the winter and this could be costly – the larger plants you see on the show bench are grown by this method. You will need to take cuttings of your plants to be grown this way now. Soft tip cuttings are the best to use and they can be as small as you like. Choose only those varieties that you wish to have on the show bench. They will need no bottom heat for rooting and can be treated quite severely throughout their initial growth. If cuttings have rooted before the end of this month, pot them into small pots – 3in (7.5cm) would be ideal – and let them grow on steadily. It will be necessary to start the training of these plants at a very early stage, and within a few weeks of rooting, when two pairs of leaves have been formed, the growing tips should be removed. The branching process will have started, and these plants will not be allowed to flower this year.

Fig 84   Taking cuttings for biennial growing.

JUNE

June is the time for considering planting out into the permanent beds, so you should mark out the well-prepared beds ready. The hardy plants should have been well hardened off by now in the cold frame, and the majority will have been in 5in (13cm) pots. Try to plant in groups of three of the same cultivar, and bear in mind that these permanent bedders should be planted deeply. Remove them from their pots and plant so that the top surface of the compost in the pot is approximately 2in (5cm) beneath the surface of the soil. Remove the plants from the pots, even if your intention is to take them back inside for protection during the winter. It is far better to leave them out, having prepared the garden well, even if the cultivars chosen are not considered to be hardy – give them the chance. Before planting out, make sure of the heights to which your plants could grow, and put the tallest at the back and the shortest in the front. Consider using standards as 'dot' plants, but remember that they must not stay out over the winter.

Plants growing as biennials will be growing well by now. Continue to pinch out all growing

87

Fig 85   Planting out hardy plants in a saucer-shaped indentation.

tips at every second pair of leaves – you must make sure that each growing tip is removed to get a symmetrical plant. These plants are stronger and grow sturdier if they are grown without the protection of glass throughout the summer. If you have an area where grass is allowed to grow, your plants placed in this environment will have the moistness around them that they like so much. When the plants are

Fig 86   Fuchsias grown under net shading.

outside keep a very careful eye open for pests and spray regularly. The capsid bug on outdoor plants is a nuisance as it causes distortion of the young growing tips.

Plants in the greenhouse will need heavy shading all the time now. Keep the vents and doors open day and night so that there is a constant stream of air through each plant. Damp down the floors and benches daily. Allow plenty of space between plants on the benches – they should not be touching each other. Continue to turn the plants (perhaps a quarter turn daily) so that there is even growth. When the first flower buds appear, perhaps towards the end of the month, either let them flower (if you require your plants purely for decorative purposes), or remove the flower buds (if you are timing them for a specific show). Don't forget the length of time necessary from the final pinch to getting the plant in full flower. Some growers remove all flowers which are out until fourteen days before the show and then let the fuchsia flower.

Keep an eye on your baskets and half baskets which can now be placed permanently outside. Remember that they will require daily attention with regard to watering and feeding. Keep an eye open for pests, especially the white fly. Early treatment will prevent a major epidemic.

You can, if you wish, continue to take cuttings. These could be useful to grow on as biennial plants, retained in 3½in (9cm) pots during the winter, but it is often found that cuttings taken during these hottest months are less easy to

Fig 87   Shaded fuchsias.

Fig 88   Hanging out baskets on sturdy wall brackets.

root. Loss of moisture both from the compost and as a result of transpiration prevents rapid rooting. The coolest spot combined with some method of retaining high humidity around the cuttings is the answer.

Continue the regular feeding. Fuchsias are gross feeders and will repay your efforts. It might not be a bad idea now to change to a feed with a different analysis – at this time of the year you should be giving a balanced food with equal proportions of nitrogen, potash and phosphates.

More and more flowers will be appearing as the month progresses, so keep a record of the dates to make plans for future years. Visit the greenhouses of other growers and try to visit as many nurseries as you can so that you can make a wider choice for another year. Don't rely on memory – make a note of the cultivars that you have seen and admired.

Fig 89   Plants in flower – on the show bench with the winning ticket.

JULY

July is the time of the year towards which you have been working. It doesn't really matter if you have been growing your plants with the intention of showing them, or whether you have been growing them purely for the pleasure they give. Flowers are everywhere.

Keep a very keen eye on your own plants and take off all old flowers as soon as they begin to look a little jaded. Remove any foliage that is becoming exhausted, as one leaf falling across a branch could easily spoil the whole plant. The more flowers you remove the more you will get.

Towards the end of the month the show scene will be getting into full swing. Visit as many as you can, taking your notebook with you. Visit the Fuchsia Society table and if there are any queries you have about any aspect of fuchsia growing do not be afraid to ask – you will find the officials only too pleased to oblige. If you are doubtful about the name of a plant you have in your collection, take along a twig of it containing flowers, buds and foliage. It is possible that somebody might recognise it, but do not be disappointed if you are unsuccessful.

If you are entering plants in a show, make sure your entry form arrives with the Show Secretary in plenty of time. Never be rushed into doing anything, whether it is arriving at the show venue or arranging your plants on the benches. It has taken a long time to produce your show plant so present it so that it is showing itself off to the best possible advantage. Any canes or ties you use to support your branches (which will be heavily laden with flowers) should be as inconspicuous as possible. Make sure that the plant is pest-free. Use insecticide pins or a systemic insecticide watered into the compost – do not spray on open flowers or well-developed buds, or they will be severely stained. Any powder residues from feeds you may have used should be carefully removed from the leaves, and a final spray with clear water when the plants are staged will give them a sprightly look. Examine all your plants carefully before leaving them, in an effort to find those seed pods hiding amongst the foliage. If possible get someone else to look for you as well, as two pairs of eyes are better than one.

If you are really adventurous, and have the space, now is the time to be thinking of hybridising. You will be able to choose the plants you wish to use as parents, as they will be showing off

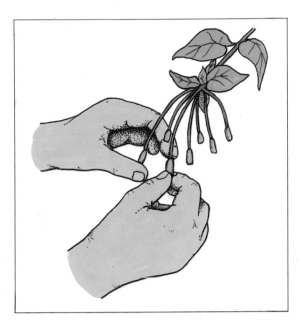

Fig 90   Collecting seed pods for hybridising.

Fig 91   'Bobby Shaftoe

Fig 92 'Lady Isobel Barnet'.

your desired characteristics now. Be patient and don't expect instant success.

Continue with regular feeding both inside and outside the greenhouse. Take care with the watering and remember that water droplets on leaves and flowers will magnify the sun's rays shining through the glass, causing unsightly scorch marks. Continue to try and handle each plant daily. Make a note of any idiosyncracies that you may see amongst your plants – some need more feed or root space than others, or object to being severely pinched. If a certain plant does not seem to want to grow for you, in spite of the fact that it grows like a weed next door, do not despair – you can try again next year if you wish or, far better really, give that plant a miss and grow those which do really well for you.

Cuttings will root now if you really need them but the higher outside temperature is not really conducive to quick rooting. Leave it until next month or even the month after when you will be in more control of the propagating temperature.

Plants out in the garden will be in full bloom. Check (for next year) that you have not planted them too close together. Keep an eye open for any pests and diseases that may be lurking out there and deal with them before they become too severe. Pick off dead flowers and seed pods to ensure a continuation of the flowering.

AUGUST

Everything is in full flower at this time of the year. Shows are in full swing, so take the opportunity to visit them – the season is short. Don't forget that record you need to keep of the cultivars that attract you – they might not have attracted the judges but that is of little importance.

The plants in the garden will welcome a regular boost of a liquid feed. Don't forget the plants in the hanging baskets, which will need regular attention. Make sure that they do not completely dry out (a regular soaking in a bucket of water will be beneficial). Remove all spent flowers, seed pods and yellowing leaves. If plants are looking a little sickly, examine them carefully as this could mean an infection of red spider mite or greenfly. Yellowing of the leaves may be as a result of magnesium deficiency, and a dose of

Fig 93   Once the baskets have been hung, they still need care and attention, with regular watering and feeding.

Epsom Salts (magnesium sulphate) will soon redress the balance.

Any flowers that you pollinated last month might be getting to the stage when the ripe berries will fall – watch them carefully. If you successfully obtain some seed, sow it straight away.

If you intend to keep a section of your greenhouse heated during the winter, cuttings taken now will grow steadily and produce some excellent plants for next year. You will be needing good, well-formed plants for planting out and in the baskets, so it might be worth considering. A minimum of 45°F (7°C) will keep them just 'ticking over'.

Plants which you are growing on the biennial system will be standing outside in their 4in (10cm) or 5in (12.5cm) pots. Don't be tempted to pot them on into larger pots even if the present pots are filled with roots. Don't allow them to flower, but keep pinching out the growing shoots and feed them with a high nitrogen fertiliser. Removal from the pots and

Fig 94   Removing dead flowers and seed pods.

93

cutting off the lowest part of the rootball before replacing with some fresh compost will keep the root system active. Make sure that these plants are kept pest-free.

At this time of the year many people are growing their fuchsias in tubs on their patios. If one really catches your eye, find out what different types of plants have been used to build up the display. If it is possible to obtain some cuttings of the plants used for foliage, do so, as they are likely to root quite easily at this time of the year. Use other plants to complement your fuchsias.

Fig 95   If you see any warning signs at all, spray immediately to combat pests and diseases.

SEPTEMBER

In September the plants are still looking fine. They are perhaps a little jaded in their pots but after a busy season they are in need of a rest. All plants should really be outside at this time of the year, to help the shoots to ripen in preparation for the winter.

Plants growing in the garden are probably looking better now than they have ever before, probably because of the heavy dews we experience during this month, and the extra humidity around them that they like so much. Most plants will be showing signs of new fresh growth – the tips of the branches will be looking a fresher green colour, and new flower buds will be forming. This second flush of growth can be of use, both from the decorative point of view in the garden and also in providing us with new cutting material.

Cuttings can still be taken – in fact, this might be considered to be the ideal time to take them to have good young plants growing away well at the very beginning of next season. Cuttings taken now will not require the assistance of any heat to root – I usually place them under the staging of the greenhouse away from the bright sun. These rooted cuttings can be allowed to develop in the late autumn and then kept 'ticking over' during the winter. They don't take up a great deal of space. When taking the cuttings try

to remove the small buds in the tips without damaging the growing shoots.

Continue to feed all of the plants with a feed containing a high level of potash, to help to ripen up the wood. It is not really advisable to pot on plants at this stage unless you can be sure that they will make a good root system around the new compost.

Keep a very wary eye open for pests and diseases. Regular spraying or the use of insecticide pins and systemic insecticides will help to keep them in check. It is too easy at this stage of the season to forget this important task. Pests which escape you now might well over-winter amongst your plants, ready to start a fresh invasion in the spring.

Continue to remove all dead flowers and seed pods. Don't be tempted to use these seed pods as seeds – although you will know the parentage of the seed-bearing plant, you will not know the pollen bearer. It would be pure luck if you obtained anything really worthwhile and much space and energy will have been used up. Make sure that any dying leaves are removed from the plants. Don't let them fall on the lower branches, as botrytis could easily set in with the moist September conditions.

Give some thought towards the end of the month to the winter storage of your plants. On a bright sunny day, with everything out of your

Fig 96 Fuchsia procumbens.

Fig 97 A good job to do in the autumn is cleaning out the greenhouse in preparation for winter.

greenhouse, you might well be tempted to give a thorough cleaning out. Cleanliness now will pay dividends later. Plan your winter storage – if you have too many of a certain cultivar decide which you will dispose of. Friends will still be pleased to receive them.

OCTOBER

In October the evenings are drawing in, the night dew is even heavier and the plants in the garden are blooming well.

It is a dangerous month and one during which you can expect the first frosts. Plants which have been standing outside can continue to do so, but do keep an eye on the weather forecast. If frost is threatened they must go under cover, although no great damage is likely to be done by

a slight frost, in fact, if anything it might well do a bit of good.

The very youngest of your plants, especially those which were rooted as cuttings during the last couple of months, will not stand any frost. Their immature shoots are very susceptible to damage, so you must make sure that they are kept in a warm position. If you have thermostatically-controlled heat then it will be wise to be using this now, on a setting that is not too high, but sufficient to keep a temperature of about 45°F (7°C). A fan heater at this time of the year is ideal for keeping the air moving.

Fuchsias out in the garden will probably be continuing to flower profusely, when other summer bedding plants have long since passed their best. It is still possible to take soft tip cuttings if you wish.

Decide what you are going to do with your

Fig 99   'Mary'.

outside plants. If you are going to leave them in the garden, it is not a bad idea to make a sketch plan now showing where your plants are situated and giving their names. It is amazing how labels disappear during the winter, and whilst you can still see the flowers you will still know the names. Any of the more tender varieties that you decide to leave outside should be the main plants from which you take some late cuttings. If

you have used standards for your bedding, be ready to take them indoors. It would be a pity to lose the plants by the stems becoming frosted. These plants take up quite a lot of space for storage, so special consideration needs to be given.

Plants which were left in their pots during the summer will need to be taken inside later. Don't be in too much of a hurry – the first frost probably will not kill them but simply help in the defoliation. Most will probably still be in full flower, so take advantage of that bonus.

Fig 98   (Preceding page) 'Blue Waves'.

Continue to keep an eye open for pests and remove them by spraying. If you have returned some of the plants to the greenhouse and pests are found it is better to kill them by using smoke cones rather than moistening the atmosphere in the greenhouse too much by spraying.

Some of the nurserymen are now beginning to send out their next season's catalogues, so make sure you get your copy. Decide which of the new varieties you wish to add to your collection.

If you have sown seeds from the plants that you hybridised, the first successful germinations will be visible. Treat them gently and pot them on as soon as they are large enough to handle. Remember that they are very erratic in their germination, so do not throw away the compost from the pot until you are sure that no other seedlings are going to appear. It is often the late arrival which makes the best plant.

NOVEMBER

November is a dangerous month for your fuchsias: many still want to continue to flower, although generally they will be showing signs of tiredness. There is no point in trying to force them to continue; encourage them to rest.

Reduce the amount of watering you give to plants which may still be outside, as the heavy night dews will be all they need. Consider bringing all the plants in under cover. Before doing so make sure that your storage area is clean and free from pests. All plants too should be free from pests and diseases so, before bringing them inside, remove all the leaves that are remaining on the plants. You may prune back some of the more straggly stems if you wish, but do not be tempted to prune too severely. When all the foliage has been removed and no debris remains on the surface of the compost, give the whole plant a thorough spraying with a mixture of insecticide and fungicide. Make sure that the plant is thoroughly soaked and give it a chance to dry off slightly before

taking it inside. Don't pack the plants together too tightly. Give them a covering of some insulating material to protect from the frosts (see Chapter 6).

Your very young plants will need preferential treatment now. They will need a temperature of 45°F (7°C) minimum to keep them just growing – you don't want them to grow fast as the light intensity is insufficient to give sturdy growth. Keep an eye open for pests and spray if the weather is conducive. On damp misty days, when the air is still and almost stagnant, do not attempt to spray.

Biennial plants will be allowed to just stay alive – don't feed or encourage growth. Any leaves which turn yellow and drop off should be removed. Some will, but do not worry, more will grow to take their place in the spring.

Outdoors the hardies will probably continue to flower. Make the most of it, but put a protection of peat around the base of the plant. The plants will probably be looking a bit straggly but don't be tempted to cut them back.

DECEMBER

December is a really quiet month with very little that can be done. Watering, if at all necessary, should be undertaken with the greatest of care, as you don't want a damp, cold atmosphere in the greenhouse. It is important however that the plants are not allowed to get bone dry – more plants are lost through this than through excessive watering.

Young plants will be looking a little fed up and you may fear that they are succumbing to the dullness of the weather. Do not worry. Maintain the minimum heat recommended, and with the increase in the daylight hours and the light intensity they will be experiencing from the end of this month, things will improve. Keep an eye open still for any pests and deal with them by means of smokes.

Also keep an eye open for any leaves which fall on to lower branches. Remove them, other-

Fig 100   'Blush o' Dawn'.

wise the shape of your plant might be severely spoilt.

If you want very early cuttings some of your stock plants can be brought back to life by spraying the branches with tepid water. Place them in the warmest part of the greenhouse. The young shoots which form can be used for the very earliest cuttings at the end of the month. Use them when they have formed just two pairs of leaves and the soft tip.

Examine the stored plants regularly and make sure that the compost is not bone dry.

Ensure that the protective covering round the base of the hardies is in position and that any dead foliage has been removed from the overhead branches.

Send off your renewal form to any societies that you may have joined – the local society and the British Fuchsia Society deserve your support.

CHAPTER 9

Recommended Cultivars

Alice Hoffman (Klese 1911) Semi-double. Tube and sepals rose. Corolla white-veined red. Foliage bronze. Excellent variety for growing in the hardy border.

Annabel (Ryle 1977) Double. Tube and sepals white. Corolla creamy white. Makes an excellent show plant, either as a bush, shrub or grown as a standard. Always an eye catcher although care must be taken in transportation – the flowers bruise very easily.

Fig 101 'Annabel'.

Ann H Tripp (Clark 1982) Single/semi-double. Tube and sepals white. Corolla white. Foliage light green. A good strong grower which makes an excellent bush shape with little training.

Auntie Jinks (Wilson 1970) Single. Tube pink. Sepals white. Corolla purple. For a basket this one is hard to beat. Flowers continuously and will rapidly fill baskets of any size.

Autumnale (Meteor 1880) Single. Tube and sepals scarlet. Corolla purple. Foliage golden-red. Semi lax growth. The beauty of the foliage gives a very attractive plant even when not in flower. Although lax in growth the branches tend to grow horizontally.

Ballet Girl (Veitch 1894) Double. Tube and sepals bright cerise. Corolla white. Large flowers. Always admired whenever seen. Makes an excellent plant for show purposes.

Bambini (Pacey 1985) Single. Tube and sepals crimson. Corolla mallow. Small flowers. Excellent for growing in window boxes or on a rockery. The small flowers make it an ideal subject for growing in small pots.

Barbara (Tolley 1971) Single. Tube and sepals pale pink. Corolla tangerine-pink. Strong upright grower which will make an excellent standard.

Billy Green (Raiser unknown 1966) Single. Tube, sepals and corolla salmon pink. Accepted as a *Triphylla* type. 'Billy Green' is so easy to grow that it should be in everybody's collection.

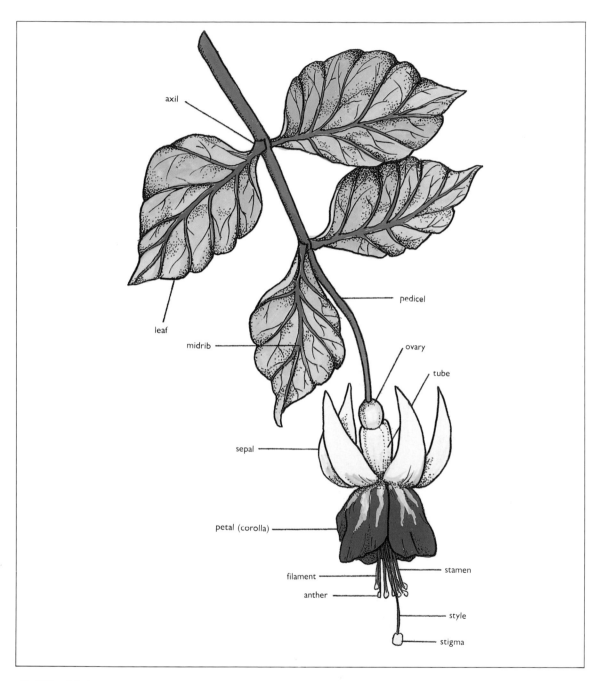

Fig 102   A fuchsia spray with its parts named.

Will make an excellent plant with a minimum of attention.

Blue Veil (Pacey 1980)   Double. Tube pure white. Sepals pure white. Corolla lobelia blue. Large blooms. Strong trailer – will make excellent basket.

Blush of Dawn (Martin 1962)   Double. Tube and sepals waxy white. Corolla silver grey/lavender blue. Large flowers. Trailing variety which makes excellent basket.

Bobby Shaftoe (Ryle-Atkinson 1973)   Semi-double. Tube clear frosty white. Sepals clear frosty white flushed with palest pink. Corolla clear frosty white. Profuse flowers of medium size.

Fig 104   A half basket of 'Border Queen'.

Fig 103   'Bobby Shaftoe'.

Bon Accorde (Crousse 1861)   Single. Tube and sepals white. Corolla pale purple. Upward-looking blooms. Strong upright grower. Grown as a standard it looks very attractive with its flowers growing upwards and away from the foliage.

Border Queen (Ryle/Atkinson 1974)   Single. Tube and sepals rhomadine pink. Corolla pale violet. Very floriferous. Well named and is indeed a queen amongst the border plants. An excellent cultivar to use on the show bench or in the hardy border.

Brutus (Lemoine 1897)   Single. Tube and sepals rich cerise. Corolla dark purple. The richness of the flowers will always enhance a hardy border. One of the earliest to flower and remains so over a long period. 18in (45cm).

Cambridge Louie (Napthen 1977)   Single. Tube and sepals pink. Corolla rose. Very floriferous, easily-shaped plant. Excellent for show work – easy to shape and always in flower. Named after a very keen fuchsia enthusiast who is blind.

Fig 105   'Carl Wallace'.

Fig 106   'Checkerboard'.

Carl Wallace (Hobson 1984) Double. Tube and sepals rosy red. Corolla violet purple. Medium-sized blooms, very free flowering.

Cascade (Lagen 1937) Single. Tube and sepals white, heavily flushed with carmine. Corolla deep carmine. An excellent cultivar for use in the basket as its name implies. One fault is that it tends to flower from the very ends of the branches, leaving long expanses of foliage.

Celia Smedley (Roe 1970) Single. Tube and sepals neyron rose. Corolla vivid currant red. Large darkish foliage. I make no secret of this being my favourite. The colouring is very distinctive and it will make an excellent upright plant quickly with a minimum of training. Very floriferous.

Chang (Hazard and Hazard 1946) Single. Tube orange red. Sepals orange/red tipped green. Corolla orange. Very floriferous small flowers. The oriental name suits this cultivar well.

Charming (Lye 1895) Single. Tube carmine. Sepals red/cerise. Corolla purple. Foliage yellowish. For the hardy border this one is hard to beat. The colour of the foliage complements the colouring of the flowers. 30in (7cm).

Checkerboard (Walker and Jones 1948) Single. Tube carmine. Sepals red shading to white. Corolla red. Strong upright growth. The very distinctive colouring of the flowers makes this cultivar easily recognisable. Its strong upright growth may encourage use as a standard, although the branches can be rather stiff.

Cloverdale Pearl (Gadsby 1974) Single. Tube white. Sepals white/pink tipped with green. Corolla white. An excellent plant for show work or in the border.

Coquet Bell (Ryle-Atkinson 1973) Single to semi-double. Short tube and sepals rose mad-der. Corolla pale mauve. Bell-shaped blooms with slightly wavy edge. Upright, free-flowering plant.

Cotton Candy (Tiret 1962) Double. Tube white with tinge of pink. Sepals white. Corolla pale pink. Dark to medium green foliage. Rather lax grower and will make good basket.

Dark Eyes (Erickson 1958) Double. Tube and sepals deep red. Corolla violet blue. The very attractive deep colouring of this plant — which holds the shape of its double flowers over a long period — makes it an excellent one to grow.

Display (Smith 1881) Single. Tube and sepals rose pink. Corolla deeper rose pink. Saucer-shaped flowers. May be used in any type of growth from small pots to large specimen plants. In the garden it makes a good round mound of flowers. 18in (45cm).

Dollar Princess (Lemoine 1912) Double. Tube and sepals cerise. Corolla rich purple. One of the first to be seen in flower.

Dusky Beauty (Ryle 1981) Single. Tube and sepals neyron rose. Corolla pale purple with pink edges. Small to medium flowers. The beginner on the show bench should try this one. An excellent, easily-shaped plant.

Empress of Prussia (Hoppe 1868) Single. Tube and sepals vivid scarlet. Corolla purple. Plant it and forget it. It will never let you down, growing to its maximum height quickly and producing a constant supply of largish flowers. 36in (90cm).

Estelle Marie (Newton 1973) Single. Tube and sepals greenish white. Corolla violet. Very attractive colouring on the many flowers produced make this a 'banker' on the show bench. Watch out, though, for flowers which produce more than four sepals.

F. Procumbens (Cunnington 1839) Tube greenish-yellow, red at base. Sepals green. No corolla. Blue pollen. Growth creeping. Hardy. A native of New Zealand. Seeds, when formed, should be left on the plant and are attractive, being much larger than the very small flowers.

Flirtation Waltz (Waltz 1962) Double. Tube and sepals creamy-white. Corolla shell pink. An excellent variety which will always produce a good supply of flowers. Care will be needed in transporting to shows as the flowers tend to bruise easily.

Foxtrot (Tolley 1974) Semi-double. Tube and sepals pale cerise. Corolla pale lavender. Use this one in pots or in the garden border. It holds its flowers over a long period.

Frank Saunders (Dyos 1984) Single. Tube and sepals white. Corolla lilac pink. This cultivar will make a very attractive plant very quickly — always seen on the show benches.

Fulgens (De Candolle 1828) Long tube and sepals a light vermilion red. Large lush green leaves. An excellent species for the beginner to try.

Garden News (Handley 1978) Double. Tube and sepals frosty pink. Corolla magenta rose. Good hardy doubles are hard to find with light colouring but this one certainly is excellent for the purpose. 36in (90cm).

Genii (Reiter 1951) Single. Tube and sepals cerise. Corolla rich violet. Foliage yellowish. One of the nicest of hardy plants with its yellow foliage beautifully complementing the richness of its flowers. 30in (75cm).

Golden Marinka (Weber 1955) Single. Tube and sepals rich red. Corolla dark red. Foliage green and yellow. Sport from 'Marinka'.

Fig 107 'Garden News'.

An excellent basket variety but a little slow sometimes to get going. Best grown to a reasonable size in pots before placing in the basket.

Harry Gray (Dunnett 1981) Double. Tube white streaked rose pink. Sepals white. Corolla white/rose pink. Always seen in baskets and half baskets. So floriferous that it is sometimes not possible to see much foliage.

Heidi Anne (Smith 1969) Double. Tube and sepals crimson. Corolla lilac. An excellent small-flowered double that produces a good symmetrical bush easily.

Herald (Sankey 1867) Single. Tube and sepals scarlet. Corolla deep purple. Foliage light green. A must for the hardy border as the light foliage and the abundance of flowers will always produce an attractive spectacle. 24in (60cm).

Jack Shahan (Tiret 1948) Single. Tube and sepals pale rose. Corolla rose bengal. Largish flowers freely produced. Rather lax growth and

Fig 108   A half basket full of 'Harry Gray'.

Fig 109   A half standard 'Joy Patmore'

will make an excellent basket in flower for a long period.

Joan Smith (Thorne 1958)   Single. Tube and sepals pink. Corolla pink/cerise. Excellent strong upright grower.

Joy Patmore (Turner 1961)   Single. Tube and sepals waxy white. Corolla rich carmine. You will rarely find a show where this cultivar does not appear. The pastel shading of its flowers produced on an easily-shaped plant makes it a 'banker' for the showmen.

King's Ransom (Schnabel 1954)   Double. Tube and sepals white. Corolla purple. A striking flower which is freely produced on a strong growing bush.

Fig 110   'Lena'.

La Campanella (Blackwell 1968) Semi-double. Tube and sepals white/pink. Corolla purple. A must for the users of baskets. Perpetually in flower and self-cleaning. Will take full sunlight. A slow starter when first struck as a cutting but makes up for lost time later.

Lady Isobel Barnet (Gadsby 1968) Single. Tube and sepals rose. Corolla rose purple. One of the most floriferous cultivars. If it has a fault it is that it produces too many flowers. Six to eight from each leaf axil is not unusual. Nevertheless an excellent cultivar.

Lady Patricia Mountbatten (Clark 1985) Single. Tube and sepals palest pink. Corolla pale lilac. The delicate colouring of this cultivar makes it very attractive. Will be seen on the show benches for a long time to come.

Lady Thumb (Roe 1966) Semi-double. Tube and sepals carmine. Corolla white. Sport of 'Tom Thumb'. For the border, the window box or patio display, this one is a must. The family – 'Tom Thumb', 'Son of Thumb', and 'Lady Thumb' – are essential for the front of the hardy border. 12in (30cm).

Lena (Bunney 1862) Semi-double. Tube and sepals flesh pink. Corolla rosy magenta flushed pink and paling at base. Growth lax bush and will make an excellent basket. Hardy. 18in (45cm).

Liebriez (Kohene 1874) Semi-double. Tube and sepals pale cerise. Corolla pinkish white. Continuous blooming. Excellent for all pot work or as a hardy plant in the garden.

Loeky (de Graaf 1981) Single. Tube and sepals rosy red. Corolla lavender fading to rose pink. Medium-sized, flat, saucer-shaped flowers.

Margaret (Wood 1937) Semi-double. Tube and sepals carmine. Corolla violet. Very strong grower. Excellent in the border for its height and perpetual flowering. 36–48in (90–120cm).

Fig 111 'Margaret Pilkington'.

Margaret Brown (Wood 1949) Single. Tube and sepals rose pink. Corolla light rose. Very prolific flowerer, and one I would always recommend. Throughout the summer plants of this cultivar drip with flowers. 24in (60cm).

Margaret Pilkington (Clark 1984) Single. Tube and sepals waxy white/pink. Corolla bishop's violet. An eye-catching cultivar.

Margaret Roe (Gadsby 1968) Single. Tube and sepals rosy red. Corolla pale violet-purple. Very free medium blooms held erect from the plant. Strong upright growth.

Marilyn Olsen (Wilkinson 1987) Single. Tube and sepals rosy pink. Corolla almost white.

Fig 112 'Mieke Meursing'.

Very floriferous and rapidly became a favourite among the showmen.

Marin Glow (Reedstrom 1954) Single. Tube and sepals waxy white. Corolla rich purple. The distinctive colouring of this cultivar will always cause it to be popular with all who see it. Easy to grow and train.

Marinka (Rozaine-Boucharlat 1902) Single. Tube and sepals rich red. Corolla darker red. The standard by which other basket variety fuchsias are measured. The rich red of its flowers contrasts beautifully with the dark green of its leaves.

Mary (Bonstedt 1894) Single. Tube, sepals and corolla vivid scarlet. Rich dark sage green foliage. Very free-flowering. Upright growth. An excellent one to use for *Triphylla* classes.

Mieke Meursing (Hopwood 1968) Single to semi-double. Tube and sepals red. Corolla pale pink veined red. Very floriferous, easily-shaped plant. This cultivar has been one of the most successful winners on the show bench since it was introduced. (The anxiety of knowing whether this one should be classified as single or semi-double on the show bench has been removed, as singles and semi-doubles can now be shown in the same classes.)

Minirose (de Graffe 1983) Single. Tube and sepals pale rose. Corolla dark rose. The smallness of the flowers make this an excellent variety for use in small pots. Flowers continuously over a very long period.

Mipam (Gubler 1976) Single. Tube and sepals pale carmine. Corolla magenta pink. Grown as a bush or shrub this plant will provide you with a perpetual bouquet of flowers.

Mrs Lovell Swisher (Evans and Reeves 1942) Single. Tube and sepals flesh pink. Corolla deep rose. This strong upright grower always produces vast quantities of medium to small flowers.

Nellie Nuttall (Roe 1977) Single. Tube and sepals bright red. Corolla white. For small pot work there is no better plant to use – the brilliance of its flowers makes it shine. Easily trained into all shapes.

Fig 113 'Nellie Nuttall'.

Orange Crush (Handley 1972) Single. Tube and sepals and corolla orange salmon. If you like the orange colours, this one must be on your list. An excellent variety which flowers over a long period. Try it out of doors.

Other Fellow (Hazard and Hazard 1946) Single. Tube and sepals waxy white. Corolla coral pink. Many small flowers make this an extremely attractive plant.

Pacquesa (Clyne 1974) Single/semi-double. Tube and sepals deep red. Corolla white. With its fairly large flowers freely produced this cultivar is always seen gracing the show bench.

Paula Jane (Tite 1975) Semi-double. Tube and sepals carmine rose. Corolla beetroot-purple maturing to ruby red. Good strong floriferous grower.

Perky Pink (Erickson-Lewis 1959) Double. Tube and sepals pink. Corolla white/pink. The medium-sized blooms are freely produced. Does well in the show class category.

Perry Park (Handley 1977) Single. Tube and sepals pale pink. Corolla bright rose. The medium-sized flowers are produced early in the season. This is a very floriferous cultivar bearing as many as six flowers in each leaf axil.

Pink Galore (Fuchsia-La 1958) Double. Tube, sepals and corolla candy pink. Dark foliage. Always sought as a good basket variety. As the individual plants are not of great size it is worth considering placing more than the usual number of plants in each basket.

Pink Marshmallow (Stubbs 1971) Double. Tube and sepals pale pink. Corolla white. Large flowers. A basket of this cultivar is very eye-catching. The large flowers are freely produced and cascade beautifully.

Fig.114   A hanging basket of 'President Margaret Slater'.

Pixie (Russell 1960) Single. Tube and sepals cerise. Corolla rosy mauve. Foliage slightly yellowish. The vigorous growth will rapidly form an excellent bush in the garden. Can be used for hedge work if required. One of the nicest varieties. 30in (75cm).

President Leo Boullemier (Burns 1983) Single. Short fluted tube streaked magenta. Sepals white. Corolla magenta blue maturing to blush pink. Medium-sized blooms.

President Margaret Slater (Taylor 1972) Single. Tube and sepals white. Corolla mauve/pink. Although rather late to come into flower this cultivar makes an excellent basket. Tends to flower at the ends of the branches but, if layered so that branches lie on top of each other, the effect is magnificent.

President Stanley J Wilson (Thorne 1968) Single. Tube and sepals cerise. Corolla rose carmine. The flowers are produced on long stalks and hang beautifully. An excellent basket produced from this cultivar is a sight to behold.

Royal Velvet (Waltz 1962) Double. Tube and sepals crimson. Corolla deep purple. Large flowers but floriferous for size. Always greatly admired whenever seen. The large double flowers are produced far more abundantly than is usual for this size of flower.

Rufus (Nelson 1952) Single. Tube and sepals and corolla bright red (sometimes referred to as 'Rufus the Red'). Strong upright grower. Very easy to grow and to shape. Will never let you down and the brightness of the flowers gives a fluorescent effect. 30in (75cm).

Saturnus (de Groot 1970) Single. Tube and sepals red. Corolla light purple. The small flowers abundantly produced make this an excellent cultivar to use in small pots. Very eye-catching.

Snowcap (Henderson 1890) Semi-double. Tube and sepals bright red. Corolla pure white. Strong grower. Many people have a great affection for this cultivar – the clearness of the red and the white always makes it stand out. Easy to train and to shape. One of the first cultivars I grew, and I would never be without it. 18–24in (45–60cm).

Son of Thumb (Gubler 1978) Semi-double. Tube and sepals cerise. Corolla lilac. Sport from 'Tom Thumb'. For the front of a border or for use in a window box this, together with 'Tom Thumb' and 'Lady Thumb', is a must. Will produce a well-shaped low bush very quickly. 12in (30cm).

Stanley Cash (Pennisi 1970) Double. Tube and sepals white tipped green. Corolla dark royal purple. Large flowers freely produced which hold their shape well over a long period. An excellent basket variety.

String of Pearls (Pacey 1976) Single to semi-double. Tube and sepals pale rose. Corolla pale purple. Beautifully named and very descriptive of its method of growth. The pearl-like flowers hang like tassels along the branches and are extremely attractive.

Swingtime (Tiret 1950) Double. Tube and sepals red. Corolla sparkling white. A basket variety *par excellence*. Perhaps the most popular of all for growing in baskets, although the growth can be rather stiff and therefore does not trail quite as easily as some. By weighting the ends of the laterals in the early stages of growth, the necessary trailing qualities can be utilised.

Taddle (Gubler 1974) Single. Tube and sepals deep rose pink. Corolla waxy white. A well-formed bush of this cultivar can easily be grown. The quantity of flowers produced over a long season will always make this a very popular variety.

Fig 116 *'String of Pearls'.*

Ting-a-Ling (Schnabel-Paskeson 1959) Tube, sepals and corolla white. Saucer-shaped flowers. The purity of white is always present and the flowers are freely produced.

Tom Thumb (Baudinat 1850) Single. Tube and sepals carmine. Corolla mauve veined carmine. Small flowers extremely free. Excellent for the front of the hardy border or in window boxes. Grow with 'Lady Thumb' and 'Son of Thumb', its two sports. 12in (30cm).

Tom West (Meillez 1853) Single. Tube and sepals red. Corolla purple. Foliage green/white/red. Excellent plant for variegated foliage. It will make an excellent well-shaped plant quite easily. Few flowers are produced, but as these are not required when exhibiting 'foliage' plants this is no drawback.

Torville and Dean (Pacey 1985) Double. Tube pale cerise. Sepals pale cerise, tipped green. Corolla almost pure white. Large blooms, which are freely produced.

Waveney Gem (Bruns 1985) Single. Tube and sepals white. Corolla pink. Very floriferous. One of the numerous 'Waveney' cultivars, all of which are very well worth growing. This one can be used for upright pot work or in baskets. Flowers continuously over a very long period and is always much admired.

Winston Churchill (Garson 1942) Double. Tube and sepals pink. Corolla lavender blue. Another show stopper. The double flowers, which are medium to large, are freely produced on a plant which is easily shaped. Not the easiest to get through the winter but new plants can be grown from early season cuttings and will flower profusely.

Tennessee Waltz (Walker and Jones 1951) Double. Tube and sepals rose. Corolla lilac. No garden should be without this one. Excellent in the centre of a border, and will repay with flowers over a long period. 20in (50cm).

Thalia (Bonstedt 1905) Single. Tube, sepals and corolla orange/scarlet. Dark foliage with purple underneath. *Triphylla* type, and one of the easiest and best. 'Thalia' tends to retain its leaves lower down better than others. Very often seen with a winning card on the show bench.

Fig 115 *(Preceding page) Torville and Dean.*

Appendices

I STARTING A COLLECTION

If you are just starting a collection it might be a good idea to visit a local show or a fuchsia nursery to see the plants in flower. You might discover that you have a particular liking for one type or colour, or perhaps a style of growth. Whatever it is that catches your imagination, do not obtain too many immediately. Concentrate on perhaps a dozen or twenty, and grow a number of each variety in as many different ways as you can. Get to know their idiosyncracies and the type of growth they like to produce – for example, those which are lax in growth will make good basket material, and certain others will grow well into the standard form.

Keep a diary at the very start of your fuchsia collecting, listing the names of your plants and their particular requirements. It is surprising how plants vary in the length of time from the final 'stopping' to the flowering date. If you become show-orientated, this information will be vital to you to ensure that your plants are in full bloom for the important day. When visiting shows, take your diary with you and make lists of those plants that you have admired, and possibly the names (and addresses if available) of the growers.

A maximum of twenty varieties would be ideal when first starting to grow – although you won't keep to that number it is a starting point. For ease of growing and success being almost assured, try the following:

Auntie Jinks, Billy Green, Border Queen, Cloverdale Pearl, Garden News, Herald, Joy Patmore, Margaret Brown, Marinka, Mieke Meursing, Phyllis, Royal Velvet, Snowcap, Swingtime, Tennessee Waltz, Thalia, Tom Thumb, Tom West, Westminster Chimes, and Winston Churchill.

Within this personal collection, I have tried to include those with single flowers, those with double flowers, those suitable for the garden and those suitable for hanging baskets.

II SOCIETIES AND SHOWS

Hopefully, as a result of your success in growing these beautiful plants you will wish to learn more about them. The best way to do this is to join one of the many societies which specialise in fuchsias around the country. A visit to your local library will give you the name of your local society, and the name and address of the secretary, from whom you will be able to obtain all the necessary information regarding their meeting places, dates and times.

Societies often have visits from speakers, and all hold an annual show in July, August or September. Do visit these shows and ask advice of the officials present. If you join a society you will not be forced to enter your plants on the show bench. No pressure is ever placed on members to do so, although everyone is encouraged to support the society in this way. It is probably true to say that only about ten per cent of the total membership of most societies do enter shows.

Having joined a local society perhaps you could be encouraged to join the National Society. The British Fuchsia Society has been in existence since 1938 and boasts a membership

Fig 117 'Border Queen'.

of around six thousand. The annual subscription is very modest and for it each member receives copies of the Society publications (at present an Annual, and two Bulletins which keep members up to date with Society news). Membership will also allow you entrance to most of the national shows organised by the society, held in locations around the country. If you decide to join before the first of February, you will be entitled to take part in the distribution of rooted cuttings. Three cuttings are sent to each member applying, with the cost covering postage and packing. Advice on your fuchsias is always available and it is possible to obtain information regarding the names of some of your plants by sending a spray of flowers and leaves to one of the experts on the subject.

The Secretary of the British Fuchsia Society is Mr Ron Ewart, 29 Princes Crescent, Dollar, Clackmannanshire FK14 7BW.

Fig 118   A callous.

III   GLOSSARY

Anther   The pollen-bearing part of the stamen.

Axil   The angle formed by the junction of leaf and stem from which new shoots or flowers develop.

Berry   The fleshy fruit containing the seeds; the ovary after fertilisation.

Biennial   The process of growing a plant one year to flower the following year.

Bleeding   The loss of sap from a cut or damaged shoot of a plant.

Break   To branch or send out new growth from dormant wood.

Bud   Undeveloped shoot found in the axils of plants – also the developing flower.

Callous   The 'scab' formed during the healing process of a cut surface. Forms at the end of a cutting before rooting commences.

Calyx   The sepals and tube together, the outer part of the flower.

Cambium   A layer of activity dividing cells around the xylem or wood.

Chromosome   Bodies consisting of a series of different genes arranged in linear fashion. They occur in the nucleus of every plant cell.

Clear stem   The amount of stem free of all growth. It is measured from the soil level to the first branch or leaf. It is of importance when growing standards or bushes.

Compost   A mixture of differing ingredients specially prepared for the growing of cuttings, plants or the sowing of seed.

Cordate   Heart-shaped.

Corolla   The collective term for the petals, the inner part of the flower.

Cultivar   A cultivated variety, a cross between two hybrids or species and a hybrid. Normally written 'cv'.

Cutting   A piece from a plant encouraged to form roots and thus produce a new plant. This is vegetative reproduction and plants produced by this method are true to the parental type.

Cyme   An inflorescence where the central flower opens first as in *F. arborescens*.

Damp down Raise the humidity of the atmosphere in the greenhouse by spraying plants, benches or paths with water.

Damping off The collapse and possible death of cuttings or seedlings, usually due to attack at ground level by soil-borne fungi.

Double A fuchsia with eight or more petals.

Emasculation The process of removing immature stamens from a host plant to prevent self-pollination, during the cross-pollination of two plants.

Feeding Applying additional plant nutrients to the compost in an effort to enhance growth or remedy compost deficiencies.

Fertilisation The union of male and female cells.

Fibrous roots Thin white roots produced from the main fleshy roots vital for the taking up of water and nutrients essential for healthy growth.

Fig 119 Fibrous roots.

Filament The stalk of the stamen.

Final stop The last removal of the 'growing tip' which a plant receives before being allowed to grow to flowering stage.

First stop The removal of the growing tip of a rooted cutting to encourage branching into the required shape.

Frost protection Maintaining a temperature above freezing point – 32°F (0°C).

Half hardy Plants which may be bedded out during the summer but will need frost protection during the winter months.

Hardy Plants that can be permanently planted in the garden.

Hybrid A cross between two species.

Hypanthium The correct term for the tube.

Internode The portion of stem between two 'nodes'. Rooting from this section is described as 'internodal'.

Lanceolate Lance-, or spear-shaped.

Leaf axil The point at which the leaf joins the stem and from which the side shoots will be produced.

Leaf node The slightly swollen area from which the leaf grows from the stem.

Mutation 'Sport' departure from the normal parent type.

N.A.S. The abbreviation used by show judges to indicate that an entry in a class is 'Not According to Schedule'. Exhibits so marked cannot be considered for an award within the show.

Node Part of the stem from which a leaf or a bud arises. When taking cuttings, roots form most readily from this point.

Nutrients The food used by the plant from the growing medium necessary for the sustaining of healthy growth.

Ornamental A term used to describe those plants which have decorative foliage. The foliage can be variegated or of a colour other than the usual green.

Ovary The part containing the ovules which, after fertilisation, swells and encloses the seeds.

Over-wintering The storage of plants during the resting period of the plants, the winter

Fig 120   Ornamental foliage.

months, so that the tissue remains alive though dormant.

Ovate   Egg-shaped.

Pedicel   The flower stalk.

Petal   A division of the corolla.

Petaloid   Smaller outer petal of the corolla.

Petiole   The leaf stalk.

Photosynthesis   The process carried out by the plant in the manufacture of plant food from water and carbon dioxide, using the energy absorbed by chlorophyll from sunlight.

Pinch   To remove the growing tips.

Pistil   The female part of the flower, consisting of the ovary, stigma and style.

Pot-bound   When the plant container is full of roots to such an extent that the plant will become starved of nutrients.

Pot back   To remove the old compost from around the roots of a plant, replacing the plant in fresh compost and a smaller-sized pot.

Pot on   To transfer the plant from one size of pot to a larger one, so that there will be a continuation in the supply of nutrients.

Potting up   Transferring a seedling or rooted cutting from its initial seed box or propagator into a plant pot.

Propagation   Increasing of stock by means of seeds or by rooting cuttings.

Pruning   The shortening of laterals or roots to enhance the shape of the plant or remove damaged portions.

Re-potting   Removing a plant from its pot, shaking off as much of the old compost as possible without damaging the roots, and replac-

Fig 121   A semi-double variety.

ing it, usually in the same size of pot and using fresh compost.

Rubbing out   The removal of unwanted side growths (for example, on a standard stem), usually in early bud stage.

Self-pollination   The transferrence of pollen from anther to stigma of the same flower or another flower on the same plant.

Semi-double   A fuchsia with five, six or seven petals.

Sepals   Normally four, which with the tube form the calyx, the outermost part of the flower.

Shading   Exclusion of some of the rays of the sun with blinds, netting or a glass colourant.

Shaping   To grow a plant into a definite shape by means of training the laterals or by selective pinching out of the growing tips.

Siblings   Offspring of the same female and male parents.

Fig 122   The stigma.

Fig 123   The style and anthers.

Single   A fuchsia with four petals only.

Species   Plants which are recognisably distinct occurring in the wild and which will breed true from seed.

Sport   A shoot differing in character from the typical growth of the parent plant, often giving rise to a new cultivar, and which must be propagated vegetatively.

Stamen   The male part of the flower, comprising the filament and anther.

Stigma   The part of the pistil to which the pollen grain adheres.

Stop   To remove the growing tip.

Striking a cutting   The insertion of a prepared cutting into a suitable rooting compost.

Style   The stalk carrying the stigma.

Systemics   Insecticides or fungicides taken up by the roots and carried into the sap of a plant, thus causing it to become poisonous to sucking insects or protected from the attack of viruses. Can also be absorbed through the foliage if applied in spray form.

Fig 124   The tube.

Fig 125   Woody growth.

Trace elements   Nutrients required by a plant to maintain steady and healthy growth (boron, copper, manganese, molybdenum and zinc).

Transpiration   Loss of water, mainly from the surface of the leaves.

Tube   The elongated part of the calyx, correctly called the hypanthium.

Turgid   The condition of the plant cells after absorption of water to full capacity.

Turning   The term used to describe the turning of a plant daily in an effort to achieve balanced growth from all directions.

Variety   Botanically a variant of the species, but formerly used to denote what is now commonly called a cultivar.

Virus   An agent causing systemic disease too small to be seen other than with powerful microscopes, but transmitted very easily.

Whip   A term given to a single stem of a plant being grown with a view to producing a 'standard'.

Wilt   The drooping of a plant, usually as a result of lack of moisture within the plant. Can be caused by disease or toxins.

Woody growth   Stems of a plant that have become thickened and brown with age. Particularly noticeable at the base of the plant.

IV FURTHER READING

Bartlett, G. E., *Fuchsias* (Crowood Press, 1988)

Beckett, Kenneth, *Fuchsias* (Aura Garden Handbooks)

Boullemier, L. B., *Fascinating Fuchsias* (Privately published, 1974)

Boullemier, L. B., *Growing and Showing Fuchsias* (David and Charles, 1985)

Boullemier, L. B., *The Checklist of Species, Hybrids and Cultivars of the Genus Fuchsia* (Blandford Press, 1985)

Clark, David, *Fuchsias for Greenhouse and Garden* (Collingridge, 1987)

Clark, Jill R., *Fuchsias* (Century Hutchinson, 1988)

Cooper, Adrian, various fuchsia booklets (Privately published)

Dale, Alan D., *An Illustrated Guide to Growing Fuchsias* (Grange Publications)

Ewart, Ron, *Fuchsia Lexicon* (Blandford Press, 1982)

Ewart, Ron, *The Fuchsia Grower's Handbook* (Blandford Press, 1989)

Goulding, E. J., *Fuchsias* (Bartholomew, 1973)

Jennings, K. and Miller, V. V., *Growing Fuchsias* (Croom Helm, 1979)

Proudley, B. and V., *Fuchsias in Colour* (Blandford Press, 1981)

Puttock, A. G., *Lovely Fuchsias* (John Gifford, 1959)

Puttock, A. G., *Pelargoniums and Fuchsias* (Collingridge, 1959)

Ridding, John, *Successful Fuchsia Growing* (Privately published)

Saunders, Eileen, *Wagtails Book of Fuchsias* (Wagtails Publications)

Thorne, T., *Fuchsias for all Purposes* (Collingridge, 1959)

Travis, J., *Fuchsia Culture* (Privately published)

Wells, G., *Fuchsias*, Wisley Handbook No. 5 (RHS, 1976)

Witham-Fogg, H. G., *Begonias and Fuchsias* (John Gifford, 1958)

Wilson, S. J., *Fuchsias* (Faber and Faber, 1965)

Wood, W. P., *A Fuchsia Survey* (Benn, 1950)

Wright, J. O., *Grow Healthy Fuchsias* (Privately published)

V SUPPLIERS OF FUCHSIAS

The following is a list of nurseries which specialise in growing fuchsias. It is not a complete list by any means but within it are those nurseries which I can recommend from personal experience. You will see advertisements from many other nurseries in gardening periodicals.

Arcadia Nurseries
Brasscastle Lane
Nunthorpe
Middlesbrough
Cleveland TS8 9EB

B. and H. M. Baker
Bourne Brook Nurseries
Greenstead Green
Halstead
Essex

J. Blythe
Potash Nursery
Hawkwell
Hockley
Essex

H. A. Brown
Mrs M. Slater
20 Chingford Mount Road
South Chingford
London E4 9AB

Fig 126   (Preceding page) Fuchsia corymbiflora.

Fig 127   A varied display of fuchsias.

Goulding Fuchsias
West View
Link Lane
Bentley
Nr Ipswich
Suffolk

Jackson's Nurseries
Clifton Campville
Nr Tamworth
Staffordshire

Kathleen Muncaster Fuchsias
18 Field Lane
Morton
Gainsborough
Lincolnshire

Carol Gubler
Littlebrook Fuchsias
Ash Green Lane West
Ash Green
Nr Aldershot
Hampshire GU12 8HL

C. S. Lockyer
'Lansbury'
70 Henfield Road
Coalpit Heath
Bristol BS17 2UZ

Oldbury Nurseries
Peter and Wendy Dresman
Brissenden Green
Bethersden
Ashford
Kent TN26 3BJ

R. J. Pacey
Stathern
Melton Mowbray
Leicestershire

J. V. Porter
12 Hazel Grove
Southport

J. E. Ridding
Fuchsiavale Nurseries
Stanklyn Lane
Summerfield
Nr Kidderminster
Worcestershire

Most of these nurseries have a postal service and all issue a catalogue describing the cultivars and species they have on offer (do try to send a stamped addressed envelope when asking for one). It is advisable to order as early as possible in the season; you will find that stocks of certain varieties which are very popular rapidly become exhausted.

Index